THE RESILIENT DECISION-MAKER

Navigating Challenges in Business and Life

ISBN   978-1-5445-0413-1   Paperback

            978-1-5445-0412-4   Ebook

LIONCREST
PUBLISHING

THE RESILIENT DECISION-MAKER

NAVIGATING CHALLENGES IN BUSINESS AND LIFE

JOSEPH
LAMPEL

ANEESH
BANERJEE

AJAY
BHALLA

DEDICATIONS

Joseph: For Estelle

Aneesh: For Divya

Ajay: For Khushi, Arya, and Raghuvir

CONTENTS

INTRODUCTION

MILTON IS TWENTY-NINE. HE IS PENNILESS.
In his short life to date, Milton has tried to build two businesses. Both have failed miserably. With two disastrous ventures at his back, he has been forced to declare bankruptcy. His credibility is in the gutter. His family, who have previously stood by him, are no longer willing to lend him more money or support him in any further entrepreneurial schemes.

Although Milton is not one to give up, at times it must seem to him that failure runs in his family. His father, Henry, is also an aspiring entrepreneur with a list of failures that easily dwarfs Milton's. Henry has failed in business no fewer than seventeen times. Following each failure, Henry has uprooted his family and moved to a new city to try again. The dashed hopes and constant turmoil have taken their toll on the family: Milton's parents have separated, and his father has abandoned the family in pursuit of elusive success.

What do you think of Milton at this point? Maybe you've already decided that he is a poor decision-maker with an unrealistic view of his own abilities. Perhaps he should curb his ambition and settle for a steady job and a life plan more suited to his talents. If that's your assessment, who would blame you? Given his litany of missteps and setbacks, Milton would arguably be lucky to attain even that much success.

In fact, Milton did try to find steady employment, but he did not settle for the quiet life. While he was trying new businesses—and failing repeatedly—he was also observing and learning. In due course, he established the Hershey Chocolate Company and never looked back. In 2018, more than seventy years after his death, the firm that bears his name still maintains a market cap of $20 billion and a 30 percent market share in its sector. Today, one can purchase Hershey's chocolate in myriad forms: the famous Hershey bar, Hershey's Kisses, Twizzlers, Reese's Peanut Butter Cups, and dozens more varieties.

If failure challenged Milton Hershey in one way, his initial taste of success presented him with a different test. His first successful company was, in fact, a caramel company. He could have stopped right there and enjoyed the life of a prosperous businessman, but he wanted to go further. To the consternation of his friends and family, he decided to sell the caramel company and focus his energies on creating the milk chocolate bar. In explaining his decision, he famously commented that "caramels are just a fad, but chocolate is a permanent thing."

In Hershey's time, chocolate was expensive to produce and had a short shelf life. He wanted to challenge the industry belief that chocolate was inevitably the preserve of the upper classes by making it affordable and available to people from all walks of life. This required him to develop a new formula and overcome numerous production problems. Eventually, however, after much trial and error, Hershey succeeded in pioneering what has become one of the most popular foods on the planet.[1]

Another remarkable facet of Hershey's life is that, while he was pursuing his entrepreneurial ambitions, he also made a point of treating his employees with dignity and respect. He built an entire town for workers at his factory. The company is still headquartered in this original home in Hershey, Pennsylvania, where most of the company's fifteen thousand employees live and work. He also founded a school for orphans in desperate need of education and gave vast sums of money to charity. By the time he passed away, little of his vast fortune remained. This time, his poverty was not due to his own shortcomings but because he had chosen to donate almost everything he owned to others.[2]

The Milton Hershey portrayed at the beginning of this introduction looks like a failure. The Milton Hershey who passed away in 1945 is one

---

1   Joël Glenn Brenner, *The Emperors of Chocolate: Inside the Secret World of Hershey and Mars* (New York: Random House, 1999).

2   Hershey Community Archives, 2018, *https://hersheyarchives.org/*.

of the most revered figures in American history. If you've ever picked up a chocolate bar, his legacy has touched your life. How did the twenty-nine-year-old Milton Hershey, broke and apparently going nowhere, become the man whose name adorns billions of chocolate wrappers around the world? That's the question on which this book is based.

Why Read This Book?

What was the secret of Milton Hershey's success? Let's address that question by examining his decisions and exploring where he was right and where he was wrong. Hershey could not have become a success without making farsighted decisions that ultimately paid dividends. Yet he also made bad decisions that cost him dearly, not only in his early life but also in his later years.

We can also take note of Hershey's willingness to learn. Failure is a ruthless yet effective teacher. Milton Hershey left school with a fourth-grade education, but he was always open to new experiences and sought to learn the lessons they held for him. Even so, trial and error did not always lead Hershey to the right business strategy. What is most striking about the arc of his life is that despite his many setbacks, he was not discouraged. In his journey from destitution to great wealth and back to voluntary poverty, he repeatedly bounced back from failure. Through thick and thin, Hershey consistently exercised resilience. Many qualities contributed to his success: he was highly intelligent, ambitious, and willing to learn. Above all, however, he was resilient.

Resilience is an underestimated yet essential quality. Read the story of a high achiever, in almost any field you can imagine, and there's a high chance that resilience features heavily. History tells us that explorers, scientists, soldiers, politicians, entrepreneurs, and CEOs all owe their success to the ability to bounce back from poor decisions and recover from setbacks that would floor most people.

For this reason, researchers long associated resilience only with exceptional individuals. Recent research, however, gives the lie to this idea. Resilience is not exclusive to high-profile individuals. Every one of us can cultivate our resilience when we face up to unexpected challenges in life and business.

Resilience takes many forms and plays a part in shaping each of our individual lives—how many of us escape unexpected challenges? In this book, we want to focus on a particular type of resilience: the resilience required in the making of decisions. As individuals, our resilience shapes our own lives. When we run enterprises or work in teams, our resilience—or lack of it—has a wider impact. It has an impact on the health of our organizations and the experience of the people we work with. In these contexts, we can justifiably speak of leadership resilience and team resilience, in addition to individual resilience.

How is resilience relevant to your life, dear reader? Perhaps you're a professional who deals with difficult situations, a businessperson faced with regular crises, or a manager deciding how to navigate organizational politics. We envisage that, even though you are good at what you do, you sometimes feel stretched to the limit of your endurance. Furthermore, like most people, you also encounter issues that require resilience in your private life.

Before we continue, let's clarify our definition of resilience. Professor Fred Luthans, a pioneer in the study of this area, defines it as the "capacity to 'bounce back' from adversity, uncertainty, conflict, failure, or even positive change, progress, and increased responsibility."[3] Gary Neville, an exceptionally successful soccer player who won eight Premier League titles, three FA Cups, and two Champions Leagues with Manchester United, where he earned the distinction of becoming one of their longest-serving players, offers a more personal definition:

> I developed a mechanism so that whatever mistakes I made, I would bounce straight back. Whatever was happening off the pitch, I could put it to one side and maintain my mental form. Call it mental resilience or a strong mind, but that is what we mean when we talk about experience in a football team.[4]

3   Fred Luthans, "The Need for and Meaning of Positive Organizational Behaviour," *Journal of Organizational Behavior* 23, (2002): 702.

4   Ellen E. Kossek and Matthew B. Perrigino, "Resilience: A Review Using a Grounded Integrated Occupational Approach," *Academy of Management Annals* 10, no. 1 (2016): 730.

Resilience is encapsulated by the idea of *bouncing back while sustaining a sense of purpose*. A resilient decision-maker engages actively with change and is determined to forge ahead, while maintaining the flexibility of mind to adapt as necessary. An unusual yet instructive comparison can be made between resilience in people and resilience in swords. Swordmakers have always struggled with the contradictory demands inherent in creating resilient blades. A good sword blade must be both flexible and tough. If it is not flexible, it may shatter when it encounters resistance. If it is not tough, it will lose its cutting edge very quickly.

Attempting to reconcile the contradiction between strength and flexibility has preoccupied both thinkers and researchers for years. Over the past two decades, research and publishing on resilience has expanded greatly. While there are many excellent contributions to the field, there's still a gap between the academic research and the practical applications.

We, your authors, spend our working lives studying decision-making by managers at the strategic and operational level. We observe dozens of people who are accustomed to making major decisions in their professional lives. Almost by definition, these are resilient individuals. If they weren't capable of performing well under pressure, they would not be in a position to make important decisions in the first place.

Paradoxically, however, the resilience that has earned them a position of responsibility also confronts them with challenges that stretch them to the limit. Sometimes these challenges are generated by their pursuit of strategic goals, such as new ventures or ambitious efforts to reshape their business operations. Others, such as difficult customers, new regulations, or cash flow crises, arise unexpectedly. We refer to the first type of challenges as **active challenges** and the second as **reactive challenges**.

In addition, we make a distinction between large challenges that consume a great deal of energy and smaller day-to-day challenges. The first type we refer to as **momentous challenges**, the second as **trivial challenges**. When we think about challenges, many of us bring to mind major problems and high-stakes decisions. Some challenges do indeed take this form, but others consist of a multitude of small problems. Individually, they seem too minor to matter. Taken together, however, they may test our resilience to the limit.

This book consists of three parts. In the first part, we'll lay the conceptual foundations, building on the latest research on resilience and illustrating our points with stories. We want you to clearly understand the different types of resilience and the different circumstances in which they're required. To this end, chapter 1 describes a typology of resilience, while chapter 2 focuses on the theory and practice of resilient decision-making.

In the second part, we will discuss the implications of resilience in specific contexts. How do we access resilience as individuals, teams, and leaders? Chapter 3 explores individual resilience, chapter 4 explains how teams form a unique ecosystem with their own resilience, and chapter 5 describes the powerful yet lonely position of the leader.

In the third part of this book, we'll turn the spotlight on you, addressing the question of how you can both *know* and *grow* your resilience. What is your current level of resilience? What are your strengths? What are your weaknesses? How can you reinforce your resilience to meet current and future challenges? In this third part, first, chapter 6 brings our day-to-day resilience into the spotlight, while chapter 7 offers a selection of exercises through which you can gauge your own levels of resilience. Finally, chapter 8 is aimed at helping you understand how to increase that resilience.

Why Resilience?

We spend a lot of time working with senior executives who come to our classrooms because they want to understand how to make better decisions. Many believe that the path to making better decisions lies purely in rational analysis of situations, leading to clear, well-defined recommendations. While this approach sounds good in theory, it is based on the assumption that we can free ourselves from human fallibility and engage in perfect rational thought while the chips are down and the pressure is on.

Many of the managers we speak to wish that this were indeed the case. Ideally, they would like decision-making to take place in a protected environment that excludes emotions such as anger, fear, and anxiety. In pursuit of this goal, they often turn to handbooks that offer advice on how to make purely rational decisions. The advice itself may be sound, but in practice it works only if the protected environment can be sustained.

Between us, we have accrued more than fifty years of teaching and research experience. As a result, we are relatively practiced at maintaining a rational outlook in the face of challenging scenarios. Yet we are only too aware that we are not infallible. For many of our students, especially those with experience of making decisions in the field, decisions often come down to split-second judgment calls, with an inevitable emotional component. Our students speak of both successes and failures, and the process of assessing the best course of action at speed. Their aim is to make the best possible decisions *under the circumstances*, and to bounce back from decisions that lead to less-than-optimal consequences. This reality is far removed from the idealized image of decision-making that is sometimes presented in the media.

The more we have discussed this with students, the more we have become aware of the gap between the relatively neat theoretical picture of decision-making and the messy reality. Following the 2008 financial crisis, we began to study how organizations and their leaders responded to the challenges posed by the recession that followed. We looked into the differences between organizations that coped well and moved forward and those that continued to struggle, even after market conditions improved. We found that the primary distinction was that those organizations that recovered quickly and developed a route toward a sustained upward curve were more resilient than those that didn't.

The more we teach, and the more we listen to those who we teach, the more we discover that there is a need for a book that discusses resilience in the face of the many unpredictable challenges inherent in any field. Our aim with this book is to fill the gap between textbook and reality. On a personal note, all three of us know the experience of going through professional and personal challenges, sometimes simultaneously. Cultivating our resilience has been key to doing so successfully. To an extent, this is the book we wish we had access to twenty years ago, before we understood the nature of resilience and the best ways to develop this vital quality.

What to Expect from This Book

Allow us to set the scene for you so you understand what you'll find in these pages—and what you won't find. We all accept that the world is unpredictable and full of unexpected challenges. Our core thesis is that these unexpected challenges test both our skill and our ingenuity. What's more, they test our ability to continue and adapt in the face of setbacks and crises, sometimes to the limit. This is why resilience plays such an important role in successful decision-making. In principle, we may have the intellectual and professional capabilities to deal with our challenges. In practice, the pressure of dealing with these challenges in an uncertain world can render these capabilities useless.

We write this book as a guide and a companion for decision-makers who must contend with numerous challenges, often under a great deal of pressure. Our aim is to help you understand and nurture your resilience so you can be effective when challenges come your way.

What we can't offer, however, is a cookie-cutter formula for dealing with challenges. Challenges come in many forms, and many books exhibit a tendency to match theoretical challenges with prepackaged solutions. This is usually too neat. Most challenges demand unique solutions. This is why decision-makers who can evaluate situations and decide on the best course of action are rare. Therefore, while we trust that following the advice in this book will lead you to improved outcomes, we do not aim to provide you with a straightforward map that will take you unerringly from point A to point B.

Take Milton Hershey, for example. Toward the end of his life, his definition of success was to give away his entire fortune. Perhaps yours involves making a career transition or starting a business, or perhaps it's something else instead. We leave it to you to define success. By the time you finish this book, we hope that we'll articulate the concept of resilience to you in a way that feels both familiar and new, and that resonates with your experience. You should be able to label and categorize the challenges you face and how you can develop your resilience to meet those challenges more effectively.

In chapter 1, we'll dive more deeply into the story of Milton Hershey and explore how resilience played a key role in some of his most pivotal decisions. Let's get started.

PART ONE

CHALLENGE AND RESILIENCE: AN OVERVIEW

CHAPTER ONE

EXPLORING RESILIENCE

AS HE FOUGHT THROUGH HIS MANY CHALLENGES, MILTON HER-shey passed through three stages common to entrepreneurs who exhibit the characteristics of resilient decision-making. First, he failed. Second, he learned from his failures. Third, he picked himself up and addressed his challenges again and again, each time with more creative energy, until he accomplished what he had set out to do.

Hershey had few formal qualifications, and family circumstances forced him into the labor market relatively early. His mother enrolled him as an apprentice at a printer's shop, a position he lost by the age of fourteen. By the time he was nineteen, Hershey had decided to open his first shop and strike out on his own. This enterprise quickly folded and, by the age of twenty-five, he had declared bankruptcy for the first time. Not a man to easily admit defeat, Hershey opened another shop in Manhattan, only to once again declare bankruptcy at the age of twenty-nine.

Confucius is reputed to have said "Our greatest glory is not in never falling, but in rising every time we fall." Most of us wish we could avoid failure altogether, which is why most mainstream texts on leadership and management are dedicated to preventing it. It is hard to argue with the proposition that avoiding the pitfalls that prevent us from succeeding is a worthy goal. Unfortunately, many books leave out something that most leaders and managers know: failing is an integral part of ultimately succeeding.

What makes Hershey's story special, and the reason why it's so central to our analysis, is that it's not simply about succeeding, or avoiding failure. It reminds us that we can recover from failure. It invites the deeper question of what inspires some people to rise from the ashes of defeat again and again and again, each time with even greater energy and determination.

This is not a new question. It has been asked by previous generations of psychologists. Most of the answers handed down to us focus on characteristics such as perseverance, hardiness, self-control, self-esteem, and emotional detachment. Interest in the topic spiked following the Second World War, when researchers observed the resilience of children subjected to challenging—sometimes appalling—circumstances.

Prior to this period, standard psychological theory stated that children are more or less consistently damaged by negative experiences such as trauma, deprivation, neglect, and abuse. The greater their pain, the more damage they were expected to sustain. This theory made sense in the context of Freudian psychoanalysis and was seemingly supported by clinical studies.

Later statistical studies, however, revealed unexpected results. While many children were indeed severely damaged by their intensely negative experiences, others who suffered similarly, or even more, did not show signs of lasting trauma as they grew into adults. Studying this data, researchers quickly made a connection between adult resilience and the resilience they observed in children. They asked why some children seemed able to bounce back from setbacks that stymied others, placing the emphasis on early childhood nurturing, good parenting, and a positive home environment.[5]

More recently, some researchers have argued that resilience has its roots not in nurture, but in nature, suggesting that the way we cope with adversity is written into our DNA. Today, a significant amount of research on resilience looks to genetics for answers. Michael Pluess, professor of developmental psychology at Queen Mary University of London,

---

5   Ernesto Caffo and Carlotta Belaise, "Psychological Aspects of Traumatic Injury in Children and Adolescents," *Child and Adolescent Psychiatric Clinics of North America* 12, no. 3 (July 2003): 493–535.

has been exploring the question of whether some of us carry a resilience gene. According to him, resilience could be a characteristic of people who do not display the biological and psychological symptoms that normally accompany stress.[6]

Research on stress predates research on resilience by several decades.[7] This is not surprising, since the impact of psychological stress on people's behavior is more readily observable than resilience, which is marked by the relative absence of stress symptoms. Nevertheless, there is a connection between the two. Literature on resilience, including this book, has benefited from the pathbreaking work of scholars such as Hans Selye, on physiological stress, Richard Lazarus, on psychological stress, and Cary Cooper, on occupational stress. A particularly useful distinction made by stress researchers is the distinction between *distress* and *eustress*.[8] *Distress* is associated with a perception of threats or other negative events, whereas *eustress* is stress associated with challenge or opportunity.

Milton Hershey's life was marked by both distress and eustress. In his early years, he dealt with many negative events that originated from situations beyond his control. As an adult, however, he actively sought out new challenges. By the time Hershey had started his caramel-making business and begun to enjoy some success, he was already in his midthirties. This is an age when many of us are beginning to settle down and fall into predictable patterns, not radically reshape our lives. The onset of middle age, however, was no barrier to Hershey's endeavors. When he produced his first chocolate products, he was thirty-seven. He met his wife at the age of forty and opened his chocolate factory at forty-eight.

Through all these challenges, some of which were thrust upon him and some of which were of his own making, Hershey repeatedly found creative ways to overcome both major and minor obstacles. For example, he met the woman who would become his wife while he was on a business trip. Forced to court her from afar, he encountered an unexpected

---

6   "Professor Michael Pluess," Queen Mary University of London, *https://www.qmul.ac.uk/sbcs/staff/michaelpluess.html.*

7   Cary L. Cooper and Philip Dewe, *Stress: A Brief History* (Oxford: Blackwell, 2004).

8   Monideepa Tarafdar, Cary L. Cooper, and Jeff Stich, "The Technostress Trifecta—Techno Eustress, Techno Distress and Design: Theoretical Directions and an Agenda for Research," *Information Systems Journal* 29, no. 1 (2019): 6–42.

problem: his lack of formal education meant that he had never mastered the art of writing letters. He solved this problem by wooing his bride-to-be using telegrams, the WhatsApp of his day. His brevity and ingenuity compensated for the lack of sophistication.

Hershey showed similar determination and creativity in resolving his most important business challenge. He set out to create a milk chocolate bar of good quality with a long shelf life that was also affordable. The process for producing milk chocolate was first developed in Europe, where it was considered to be a luxury product. The main challenge was the short shelf life: the product became rancid unless it was consumed shortly after production. Hershey could have reproduced the process, but he wasn't content with the idea of selling milk chocolate from his own premises for immediate consumption. He wanted both to make milk chocolate and to turn his formula into a bar that could be transported long distances. He saw an opportunity to take advantage of mass marketing and to reach an enormous audience with his invention.

While he was struggling to develop a chocolate bar that could be mass-produced, even his own wife thought he was crazy. She told him he ought to have his head examined. Many of his peers in the confectionery industry told him that developing a chocolate bar for mass-production was an impossible task. Hershey could have heeded their advice and quit while he was ahead. At this stage, he had already built a successful caramel company. He could have told himself that was good enough. But Hershey did not settle. He wasn't content with the success he already had.

It took him more than a year to find the right formula for his chocolate bar. First, he tried boiling milk in a vacuum, then in an open kettle. He experimented with different combinations of milk and sugar. Many of his concoctions tasted delicious when they were fresh but went bad after a couple of weeks. For Hershey's purposes, that wasn't good enough.

As we now know, he eventually managed to perfect his recipe. When he embarked on his quest, however, he didn't know whether he would ever succeed, or how long it might take. Along the road, he encountered many failures and setbacks. Hershey kept himself going by drawing on his formidable reserves of resilience.[9]

---

9   James D. McMahon Jr., *Built on Chocolate: The Story of the Hershey Chocolate Company* (Los Angeles: General Publishing Group, 1999).

After creating the chocolate bar and building his second company, Hershey decided to take on the challenge of building a town for his workers to live in. He poured his energy and financial resources into this project, eventually founding a town that became a stable home for his workers and a powerful element of his legacy. The town still stands today, having survived the Great Depression and all the other social, economic, and political problems that beset the United States in the intervening years.[10]

Sadly, there was one challenge not even Milton Hershey could overcome. When his wife fell ill, he traveled the world in search of a cure for her, without success. Even in the face of this tragic loss, however, Hershey showed spirit. He continued to run his business and remain in public life, eventually distributing almost his entire vast fortune to worthy causes such as the Milton Hershey School.[11] Though not all challenges can be overcome, Milton Hershey demonstrated an incredible resilience in the way he approached the many adverse situations in his life. Dogged by both professional and financial failure, and later personal tragedy, he repeatedly rose above his circumstances and found a way to move forward.

Types of Challenges

One of the fundamental messages of this book is that, sooner or later, things will go wrong. Whatever we do, however we choose to live, we will face setbacks. This is true whether we take huge risks or attempt to live as safely and conservatively as possible. The first pillar of resilience is accepting that challenges are unavoidable. Instead of constantly seeking to anticipate challenges, or trying to avoid them, we're wiser to understand how things can go wrong, what their impact can be, and how to shape our decision-making processes in the face of challenge.

As Milton Hershey's story illustrates, not all challenges are created equal. In this book, we categorize challenges by dividing them in two ways: our first distinction is between **momentous** and **trivial** challenges;

---

10   "M. S. Hershey Dead; Chocolate King, 88," *New York Times*, October 14, 1945, 44.

11   James D. McMahon Jr., "It Was Kitty's Idea," *Women-CONNECT* (Spring 2010; repr., Milton Hershey School, *https://www.mhskids.org/news/it-was-kittys-idea/*).

the second is between **active** and **reactive** challenges. These combine to create four types of challenge: **momentous active**, **momentous reactive**, **trivial active**, and **trivial reactive**.

Momentous challenges are major events with the potential to shake the very foundations of our lives, such as losing a job or the death of a loved one. Trivial challenges, on the other hand, are relatively minor. They upset us, disrupt us, but they don't radically alter our lives. An example of a trivial challenge would be a tricky work scenario, complicated by office politics, or an ongoing feud with a neighbor. Although these types of challenges aren't especially serious, they can be hard to respond positively to and easily drain large portions of our emotional resources.

Active challenges are those we choose to bring into our lives. For example, moving to a new country or setting up a new business. The latter requires steadiness as we navigate the process of completing paperwork and complying with rules and regulations. Reactive challenges happen *to* us: if the company we work for relocates, leaving us with a choice of redundancy or moving across the country, that's a reactive challenge.

A TYPOLOGY OF CHALLENGES

	MOMENTOUS	TRIVIAL
ACTIVE	**Momentous-Active** Eg.: launching a new product line, taking a job overseas	**Trivial-Active** Eg.: dealing with a safety inspection, rearranging travel plans
REACTIVE	**Momentous-Reactive** Eg.: confronting a severe recession, fighting a lawsuit	**Trivial-Reactive** Eg.: meetings that drag on, nuisance emails

While challenges to our decision-making process are an inescapable part of life, not every type of challenge is created equal. You may wish to picture trivial and momentous challenges as bricks and boulders. Life throws bricks at us all. We can deal with one brick, even two or three, relatively easily. When we see a boulder heading toward us, however, we know that we need to tackle it as a matter of urgency—or wind up squashed beneath it!

As we'll discuss in greater depth throughout this book, we draw on different types of resilience to meet different challenges. When we understand the distinct types of challenges we're likely to face, we're in a stronger position to calibrate the resources we need to respond effectively.

Milton Hershey's Resilience in Action

Let's look once again at Milton Hershey's life story, this time breaking down the challenges he faced into trivial and momentous, active and reactive.

In his early life, a lot of the challenges that shaped him were *reactive*: these challenges were thrust upon him. He was a child, so he didn't have a lot of influence in determining what happened to him. His family moved around a lot, and he lacked a strong grounding in education. Therefore, he didn't have a secure social life. This led to a number of *trivial reactive* challenges—such as his inability to compose love letters to his beloved.

The young Milton also watched his father, the primary breadwinner, fail repeatedly in his entrepreneurial pursuits. Ultimately, this led to his father declaring bankruptcy and his parents separating. Milton could do nothing about the unfolding of these series of *momentous reactive* challenges. All he could do was come to terms with them in the best way he knew how.

As an adult, Hershey made the decision to create his own business, as opposed to seeking out a steady job. Despite his early failures, he stuck to this path, learning from his failures and eventually becoming highly successful. This was an active choice on his part: he decided to bring these *momentous active* challenges into his life again and again, even when he had already tasted success.

Hershey also had his share of *trivial active* challenges. At the age of twenty-nine, when he was attempting to raise money to start his third business, Hershey approached his bank for a loan. With his poor track record, however, he was unsurprisingly rejected. Yet Hershey responded by presenting his business plan in such a convincing fashion that the bank manager chose to personally lend him the money he needed to get his business off the ground.[12] In the face of disappointment, Hershey found the resilience to be creative and convincing.

Resilience often consists of the difference between the willingness to take on new challenges and allowing painful experiences to make us risk-avoidant. Without resilience, it is difficult to reflect on our mistakes and understand where we went wrong. We may default to avoiding similar situations, limiting our capacity to express our full potential. When we are resilient, as Milton Hershey was, we can look our failures square in the face, ask ourselves what exactly went wrong, and determine what we can do differently next time. In the following chapter, we will develop this idea of decision-making in the face of challenges.

---

12   Hershey Community Archives, 2018, *https://hersheyarchives.org/*.

Key Takeaways from This Chapter

- As decision-makers, we face challenges of different types and magnitudes. Picture **trivial challenges** and **momentous challenges** as bricks and boulders. One thing we can be sure of is that life and work will throw bricks at us. When faced with one brick, or even two, we can manage them easily, although many in rapid succession may wear us down. Boulders are different. When a boulder comes rolling down the hill, it presents a major challenge that we need to tackle as a priority.

- Some challenges come upon us unexpectedly. They may not result from our own actions, but we must deal with them, whether we wish to or not. These are **reactive challenges**. Other challenges stem from our behavior. We must deal with them if we wish to attain our goals. These are **active challenges**. Understand that some challenges emerge from circumstances beyond your control, while others result from your specific decisions.

- The mainstream view of business challenges is predominantly to design strategies to preempt reactive challenges. Recognize that this is not entirely possible and acknowledge that you will need resilience to address the consequences of unforeseen challenges. Resilient decision-making begins with the understanding that our initial response to challenges may not deliver the results we seek, but that we will adapt and learn as we persist.

CHAPTER TWO

RESILIENT DECISION-MAKING

Today, Starbucks is a household name, with a coffee shop in every major town. Few people realize, however, how close Howard Schultz came to never realizing his dream of buying and growing the chain.

In 1987, Schultz was preparing to purchase Starbucks, which was then a small coffee brewing operation in Seattle. Schultz had multiple investors on board, each of whom had agreed to finance a piece of his dream, and the deal had almost reached completion. Shortly before Schultz signed the deal, however, one of his early investors tried to move the goalpost. The investor wanted to finance the entire deal himself, with no one else on board. Worse, the investor, who was very influential in the region, aggressively pushed his version of the deal, telling Schultz that if he didn't accept the new terms, he—Schultz—would never work in Seattle again.

This was a major blow. Schultz feared that if he did not accept the investor's terms, the business he was working so hard to start would never come into being. On the other hand, he knew that if he submitted to the investor's terms, he would lose control of the company. Starbucks might exist, but it would not be the company he dreamed of creating. In his book *Pour Your Heart into It: How Starbucks Built a Company One Cup at a Time*, Schultz describes the pressure he was under:

If I had agreed to the terms the investor demanded, he would have taken the dream away from me. He could have fired me at whim. He could have dictated the atmosphere and values of Starbucks and the passion, commitment, and dedication would have all gone away.[13]

Schultz was frustrated. He had wanted to pursue *his* dream, not the vision of someone else who held the purse strings. Suddenly, he was face-to-face with a seemingly insurmountable obstacle. He needed to find alternative funding—and fast. Schultz threw himself into the search. Within two weeks, he found a group of investors to cover the $3.8 million hole that saying no to the would-be sole financier left in his financing package. The deal was back on the table, and Schultz's vision was back in play.

Resilience in Decision-Making

Imagine you are a police commander in charge of a hostage-taking situation. The hostage takers have already executed one hostage, and they are threatening to shoot more if their demands are not met. You are confronted with what decision-making experts call "hard" or "impossible" decisions: there are no easy answers.

You can order your team to storm the site, knowing that it's very likely your actions will lead to casualties. You can give the hostage takers what they want, which will feel like a defeat, or you can play for time. As you try to imagine how you would react, consider these two factors: the cognitive burden of the decision, and the emotional burden.

The cognitive burden is the analytical cost of your choice. To arrive at a decision, you must gather information, analyze multiple factors, and map scenarios, all while embroiled in a tense, dynamic situation. The emotional burden can be found in the weight of your responsibilities. As you choose your course of action, you must contend with the possibility of negative consequences to others and yourself.

For example, you may need to live with the guilt of making a decision that contributes to the death or injury of innocent people. Should you give in to the hostage takers, you may need to live with a sense of

---

13   Howard Schultz and Dori Jones Yang, *Pour Your Heart into It: How Starbucks Built a Company One Cup at a Time* (New York: Hyperion Books, 1997), 92.

shame and failure. Those are only the internal consequences. Even if you believe that you made the right decision under the circumstances, you may still incur disapproval and criticism from people you respect.

This is where resilience becomes essential. A resilient decision-maker is able to make effective decisions in spite of these cognitive and emotional burdens. Even more importantly, a resilient decision-maker is capable of bearing the negative consequences of their past decisions, while learning from any mistakes and continuing to make decisions effectively. A less resilient decision-maker, in contrast, is unlikely to continue making effective decisions following setbacks. What accounts for this difference?

One theory, which goes a long way toward explaining this distinction, comes from Professor Stevan E. Hobfoll of Rush University Medical Center, Chicago, Illinois. Hobfoll's conservation of resources theory argues that we all strive to retain, protect, and build psychological resources.[14]

As the above example of the police commander illustrates, both cognitive and emotional resources are essential when dealing with challenges. We need cognitive resources to evaluate the challenges we confront and decide on the best course of action. We also need emotional resources to cope with the potential consequences to ourselves, to others, and to the organization we represent.

Resilient decision-makers succeed in retaining sufficient cognitive and emotional resources in the aftermath of setbacks, problems, or even opportunities, enabling them to rise to future challenges. In other words, they bounce back from challenging situations.

Hobfoll's conservation of resources theory is based on four principles that can be used to explain how decision-makers retain cognitive and emotional resources, and how low levels of these resources lead to poor decisions.[15] We'll briefly explore these principles.

---

14   Stevan E. Hobfoll, "Conservation of Resources: A New Attempt at Conceptualizing Stress," *American Psychologist* 44, no. 3 (March 1989): 513–524.

15   Stevan E. Hobfoll, Jonathon Halbesleben, Jean-Pierre Neveu, and Mina Westman, "Conservation of Resources in the Organizational Context: The Reality of Resources and Their Consequences," *Annual Review of Organizational Psychology and Organizational Behavior* 5, no. 1 (2018): 103–128.

The first is the **primacy of loss principle**. When confronting a challenge, decision-makers focus more on resource losses than resource gains. If they see the challenge as a particularly difficult one, they are likely to reduce, rather than increase, cognitive effort. As a result, they may opt for a standard solution, rather than seeking a creative solution. If the potential consequences of addressing the challenge are highly negative, decision-makers will likely focus on the drains to their emotional resources, not on the emotional gains they stand to reap by dealing successfully with the challenge.

The second is the **resource investment principle**. To prevent the loss of valuable resources, we need to invest in cognitive and emotional resources. To successfully replenish cognitive resources, we must cultivate a lifelong interest in learning and skill acquisition. To sustain our emotional resources, we must nurture our personal relationships with, for example, a supportive spouse, close friends, colleagues, and other members of our community.

Many decision-makers in positions of responsibility do this instinctively. Many, however, do not. This is perhaps because positions of responsibility often crowd out home life, friendships, and other activities that build relationships but that may be perceived as nonessential.

The third principle is the **gain paradox principle**. Conservation of resources theory highlights the fact that decision-makers, when dealing with challenges that rapidly consume their cognitive and emotional resources, must place greater importance on generating more of these resources.

The paradox comes from the tendency for decision-makers to undervalue both cognitive and emotional resources prior to the acceptance of a challenge, failing to build their reserves in advance. When they find themselves in the thick of a challenge, therefore, they often find themselves seeking out new resources. This principle plays a role in explaining why decision-makers dealing with challenging business problems may embark on a course of action thinking they have the resources to handle a situation themselves, only to discover that they need help and hire a consultant.

The same pattern holds true for emotional resources. Decision-makers may neglect the development of emotional resources before challenges arise, then struggle when they confront situations that place them under heavy emotional burdens. In the midst of difficulty, they may find themselves returning to and reactivating relationships that provide them with emotional support. Whether they receive the support they desire may depend on how strong these relationships were initially, prior to their neglect.

The fourth and final principle is the **desperation principle**. What happens when a person's cognitive and emotional resources are too low for the person to deal effectively with a challenge? Conservation of resources theory argues that when people are overstretched or exhausted, they may become defensive, aggressive, and irrational. Decision-makers who operate under these conditions run the risk of making fundamental mistakes. Resilient decision-makers are more likely to avoid this error; aware that they are low on cognitive and emotional resources, they will fight the temptation to act out of desperation, and instead work to replenish their resources.

Staying in the Resilient Decision-Making Zone

Proponents of rational decision-making argue that we should seek to separate our cognitive resources and our emotions. For them, emotions confuse otherwise clear analyses and make a mess of the orderly steps that, in theory, take decision-makers from analysis to action.

In reality, however, we inevitably bring both cognitive and emotional resources to our decision-making. Actions have consequences that elicit emotions, so it is hard to conceive of any action that is not motivated or colored by emotion. The danger to effective decision-making comes not from failing to separate the cognitive and the emotional, but from neglecting to take into account how they connect.

As we discussed earlier, handling challenges consumes both cognitive and emotional resources. When we have enough of both to address our challenges with ease, we may not give our resilience levels a great deal of consideration. Should our resilience levels be insufficient to handle a challenge, however, we will quickly notice our lack of resilience.

At this point, as the burden on our cognitive and emotional resources increases, our resilience levels act as a multiplier. If they are high, our effectiveness will increase and we can generate additional resources with relative ease. If they are low, on the other hand, our struggles will contribute to our frustrations, draining our resilience further.

Success will seem more elusive and doubts will creep in, increasing the difficulty of concentration and making it harder to find effective solutions. In the parlance of resource conservation theory, this leads to "resource loss cycles." An individual with low resources experiences the loss of resources more acutely, thereby leading to a spiral in which an initial loss of resources results in further losses. At its worst, this spiral leads decision-makers into the desperation principle described above.

For all its usefulness, conservation of resources theory does not explore how the desperation principle relates to decision-making. To find that out, we must turn to research on decision-making. Here we find that decision-makers who are unable to pull out of this spiral tend to respond in one of two ways. The first is to become paralyzed and enter a state of decision-making avoidance. The second is to seek escape by taking a hasty, poorly conceived decision that will not prove effective but will relieve the decision-maker of the pressure to act.

Professor Christopher Anderson of the University at Albany, State University of New York offers three reasons why we may succumb to paralysis and avoid making decisions.[16] First, we may want to maintain the status quo when we cannot see favorable alternatives to an existing situation. This may be a misleading assessment of the situation. When our cognitive resources are at a low ebb, we find it difficult to assess the situation objectively and determine whether superior alternatives are available. Second, we may slow down the decision-making process because we dread the consequences of failure. When negative consequences come into view, we avoid decisions completely. The third reason is that we may defer making a decision in the hope that a single, clearly superior option will emerge. In extreme cases, research tells us that decision-makers who do not have the cognitive resources to evaluate their situation may avoid or delay decisions until they feel they can effectively process the relevant information.[17]

16   Christopher J. Anderson, "The Psychology of Doing Nothing: Forms of Decision Avoidance Result from Reason and Emotion," *Psychological Bulletin* 129, no. 1 (2003): 139–167.

17   Samina Karim, Timothy N. Carroll, and Chris P. Long, "Delaying Change: Examining How Industry and Managerial Turbulence Impact Structural Realignment," *Academy of Management Journal* 59, no. 3 (2016): 791–817.

At the other end of the spectrum, we encounter the temptation to speed up the decision-making process in an effort to eliminate the pain of uncertainty. Professor Paul Nutt, of Ohio State University, examined over four hundred strategic decisions.[18] According to his results, only one decision in ten is truly urgent, and only one in a hundred is triggered by a crisis demanding prompt action.

In spite of this ratio, some decision-makers press ahead, even when their rushed decisions are only leading them into failure. Professor Nutt's observations on this phenomenon deserve to be quoted in full:

> The desire for speedy action has several origins. Like most humans, decision-makers fear the unknown. Decision-making can be a lonely endeavor in which a longing to meet responsibilities and worries about a failure to do so elicit fears. Such fears prompt rapid action, making it difficult to wait for alternatives to emerge.[19]

Fear eats into our emotional resources, while low cognitive resources make it difficult for us to persist with our search for alternatives. The resilient decision-maker has the emotional resources to endure fear while waiting for better options to emerge, coupled with the cognitive resources to actively search for those options.

President Kennedy's Resilient Decision-Making

President John F. Kennedy's adept handling of the Cuban Missile Crisis provides a potent example of a decision-maker in a high-pressure situation who manages to avoid the twin traps of paralysis and hasty decision-making—in a situation where the stakes could hardly have been higher. One false move could have led the world into thermonuclear war.

In October 1962, President John F. Kennedy and his advisers learned that the Soviet Union was shipping nuclear missiles into Cuba. Had the Soviets established a nuclear foothold in Cuba, they would have been in a position to launch a strike on American cities, especially those in the south of the country.

---

18   Paul C. Nutt, "Expanding the Search for Alternatives during Strategic Decision-Making," *Academy of Management Executive* 18, no. 4 (November 2004): 13–28.

19   Nutt, 14.

Although President Kennedy knew that he couldn't allow the USSR to operate nuclear bases on his doorstep, he also understood that an attack on Cuba could precipitate a full-scale nuclear conflict between the United States and the USSR. His top military commanders told him that he must call in an airstrike and bomb nuclear weapon storage sites in Cuba before the missiles became operational. This would have defused the immediate threat, but it could have had horrifying consequences. If Soviet personnel had been killed in an attack of this nature, it would have triggered retaliation that probably would have resulted in full-scale war.

Upping the pressure even further was the legacy of an event that took place approximately eighteen months prior to the Cuban Missile Crisis. The Bay of Pigs fiasco was an ill-conceived covert operation to unseat Fidel Castro. It went horribly wrong, exposing the president to a very public humiliation.

In the lead-up to the Bay of Pigs, President Kennedy felt that he had placed too much faith in the decision-making capacities of others. He did not wish to make the same mistake again. He was aware, however, that his top commanders regarded him as inexperienced and indecisive. Therefore, he confronted a double burden: he knew that he risked damaging the strategic interests of the United States, or even sparking a war that would kill millions, and he also knew that many members of his team doubted his judgment.

Despite these multiple pressures, Kennedy found the emotional resources to resist the urge to act too quickly. When he examined his generals' initial analysis of the situation, he believed that it was excessively simplistic. He was convinced that there were other options that didn't require either a preemptive strike or accepting the presence of Soviet missiles in Cuba.

During this process, Kennedy displayed great resilience. First, he slowed down the process of decision-making. Aware of the risks of committing to a course of action based on an emotional response, Kennedy gave his team time and space to generate alternatives, and he pushed them to do so.

Kennedy's approach is now considered a textbook example of good decision-making. To defuse the insistence of his military commanders, he assembled a team of people he trusted to search for new alternatives. This allowed him to shape the process, slowing it down while the team brainstormed.

Eventually, this team came up with a fresh idea: blockading the delivery of offensive weapons to Cuba. In international law, a blockade is an act of war, so the team decided to frame it instead as a "quarantine." To bolster the legitimacy of this position, the United States engaged the United Nations Security Council to make its case. This move put the ball firmly in the USSR's court: would they move past the blockade, triggering an arguably justified military response, or would they turn back? Through informal channels, Kennedy combined the stick of the blockade with the carrot of a secret sweetener: the United States would dismantle its missiles in Turkey if the Soviets removed theirs from Cuba. The Soviets agreed, and the crisis was resolved.

What can we learn about resilient decision-making from Kennedy's handling of the Cuban Missile Crisis? Fortunately for the world, Kennedy was operating with ample cognitive and emotional resources. He owed his cognitive resources to excellent formal education and to the experience he gained as a congressman. His emotional resources stemmed from the strong support he received from his family, including his brother, Bobby Kennedy, who was always by his side. By calling on these resources, Kennedy succeeded in pulling off a difficult balancing act in some of the most trying circumstances imaginable. He resisted the temptation to rush into a decision, while simultaneously offsetting the risk of sinking into paralysis.

Kennedy could have stomped his foot and acted rashly, perhaps driving the world to war. He could have dithered, allowing the magnitude of his situation to overwhelm him. Instead, he took control of the process, moving it forward and taking care not to accelerate it.

It is important to note that while Kennedy was blessed with a high degree of both cognitive and emotional resources, many of us have more of one or the other. For many, this is a counterintuitive concept. We tend to think that people are simply smart (or dumb). In fact, it's possible to be extremely high in either emotional resources or cognitive resources, while being low in the other. For example, think of a reclusive professor who struggles in social situations. He may be brilliant in his chosen field yet find it difficult to relate to a range of different people. At the other extreme, people who care for an elderly relative may draw on enormous emotional resources without having a lot of specialized knowledge—although their cognitive resources will no doubt be adequate for the tasks they perform.

Those who are high in both emotional and cognitive resources will fare well in a broad range of challenging scenarios. People who are high in *either* emotional or cognitive resources can function successfully in certain roles, albeit in a more limited range than those who have both. Those who are low in both emotional resources *and* cognitive resources are likely to struggle. In the following section, we'll explore some more examples of resilience and mine them for lessons.

Howard Schultz Remodels Starbucks Again

Let's wrap up this chapter by revisiting the career of Howard Schultz. Following the global financial crisis of 2008, Schultz had relinquished his duties as CEO of Starbucks. Watching from the sidelines, he saw a behemoth that was betraying his original vision. He felt that—with more than thirteen thousand outlets—the chain had become too large, losing its unique identity and becoming like any other coffee house.

Schultz wrote an impassioned email to the CEO, Jim Donald, and copied in his executive team. In the missive, he outlined several issues that he considered pressing, such as the loss of the small café culture he had always sought to cultivate and the watering down of the customer experience. Somehow, the email was leaked. Numerous media outlets picked it up and it was published, word for word, in the *Wall Street Journal*. Starbucks stock was hit hard.

Meanwhile, the company's board questioned Schultz's role. They spoke to him and asked him to define his role. Was he willing to let go of the company he had built, or did he want to come out of retirement and resume his role as CEO? Schultz chose the latter. He came out of retirement for a dollar a year, with the intention of rebuilding the original Starbucks vision.

Over the eleven years that followed, up to 2017 when he retired again, Schultz built Starbucks into an incredible success story. Today, the chain operates in more than fifty thousand locations, while retaining the atmosphere of a local coffee house. From his initial emotional response to what he saw as the denigration of his vision, Schultz exercised tremendous emotional and cognitive resources to turn the situation around.

Howard Schultz's Email to His Executive Team

Subject: *The Commoditization of the Starbucks Experience*

As you prepare for the FY 08 strategic planning process, I want to share some of my thoughts with you.

Over the past ten years, in order to achieve the growth, development, and scale necessary to go from less than 1,000 stores to 13,000 stores and beyond, we have had to make a series of decisions that, in retrospect, have lead [*sic*] to the watering down of the Starbucks experience, and, what some might call the commoditization of our brand.

Many of these decisions were probably right at the time, and on their own merit would not have created the dilution of the experience; but in this case, the sum is much greater and, unfortunately, much more damaging than the individual pieces. For example, when we went to automatic espresso machines, we solved a major problem in terms of speed of service and efficiency. At the same time, we overlooked the fact that we would remove much of the romance and theatre that was in play with the use of the La Marzocca machines.

This specific decision became even more damaging when the height of the machines, which are now in thousands of stores, blocked the visual sight line the customer previously had to watch the drink being made, and for [*sic*] the intimate experience with the barista.

This, coupled with the need for fresh roasted coffee in every North America city and every international market, moved us toward the decision and the need for flavor locked packaging. Again, the right decision at the right time, and once again I believe we overlooked the cause and the affect [*sic*] of flavor lock in our stores. We achieved fresh roasted bagged coffee, but at what cost? The loss of aroma—perhaps the most powerful non-verbal signal we had in our stores; the loss of our people scooping fresh coffee from the bins and grinding it fresh in front of the customer, and once again stripping the store of tradition and our heritage?

Then we moved to store design. Clearly we have had to streamline store design to gain efficiencies of scale and to make sure we had the ROI on sales to investment ratios that would satisfy the financial side of our business. However, one of the results has been stores that no longer have the soul of the past and reflect a chain of stores versus the warm feeling of a neighborhood store. Some people even call our stores sterile, cookie cutter, no longer reflecting the passion our partners feel about our coffee.

In fact, I am not sure people today even know we are roasting coffee. You certainly can't get the message from being in our stores. The merchandise, more art than science, is far removed from being the merchant that I believe we can be and certainly at a minimum should support the foundation of our coffee heritage. Some stores don't have coffee grinders, French presses from Bodum, or even coffee filters.

Now that I have provided you with a list of some of the underlying issues that I believe we need to solve, let me say at the outset that we have all been part of these decisions. I take full responsibility myself, but we desperately need to look into the mirror and realize it's time to get back to the core and make the changes necessary to evoke the heritage, the tradition, and the passion that we all have for the true Starbucks experience. While the current state of affairs for the most part is self-induced, that has lead [sic] to competitors of all kinds, small and large coffee companies, fast food operators, and mom and pops, to position themselves in a way that creates awareness, trial [sic] and loyalty of people who previously have been Starbucks customers. This must be eradicated.

I have said for 20 years that our success is not an entitlement and now it's proving to be a reality. Let's be smarter about how we are spending our time, money and resources. Let's get back to the core. Push for innovation and do the things necessary to once again differentiate Starbucks from all others. We source and buy the highest quality coffee. We have built the most trusted brand in coffee in the world, and we have an enormous responsibility to both the people who have come before us and the 150,000 partners and their families who are relying on our stewardship.

Finally, I would like to acknowledge all that you do for Starbucks. Without your passion and commitment, we would not be where we are today.[20]

We could say that, in both of the situations we've described, Schultz should have seen his challenges coming. Why couldn't he see that the investor was a shark? Why did it take him so long to realize that Starbucks was on a path that went against what he stood for?

While it would be easy to apportion blame, mistakes are inevitable. In an imperfect world, composed of imperfect individuals operating according to imperfect information, the idea that we can avoid making mistakes is the antithesis of resilience. In reality, the path to successful decision-making success is not straightforward. The real question is not whether we can avoid mistakes entirely, but whether we can bounce back from those mistakes.

20   "The Commoditization of the Starbucks Experience," Starbucks Gossip, last modified February 14, 2007, http://starbucksgossip.typepad.com/_/2007/02/starbucks_chair_2.html.

Key Takeaways from This Chapter

- Cultivate resilience, not infallibility. We all make mistakes, but resilience enables us to bounce back from mistakes. Resilient thinking begins with the understanding that things will go wrong, but they can be put right.

- Effective decision-making depends on sufficient **cognitive and emotional resources** for the task at hand. Cognitive resources enable us to analyze our challenges; emotional resources allow us to cope with the potential negative outcomes of pursuing a definite course of action.

- Resilience acts as a multiplier of resources. When we're resilient, we find ways to generate more cognitive and emotional resources, thereby bouncing back rapidly from setbacks and crises.

- The reverse is equally true. When we lack resilience, we find it harder to access the resources we need to address a challenge. This can lead us into a downward spiral. Decision-makers in this situation are prone to decision paralysis or to making hasty decisions with negative consequences.

- As individuals, we have varying degrees of cognitive and emotional resources available to us as we face up to challenges and make decisions. Some of us are strong in cognitive resources and weak in emotional resources, or vice versa, while others are strong in both or, unfortunately, weak in both.

PART TWO

RESILIENCE IN ACTION

CHAPTER THREE

INDIVIDUAL RESILIENCE

W E'VE DESCRIBED RESILIENCE—THE ABILITY TO BOUNCE BACK in the face of challenges—and why it's important. We've discussed how resilience has an impact on decision-making, and categorized challenges as momentous or trivial, active or reactive. Now, let's examine how individuals rebound in the face of challenge by looking at an experience with which most of us can identify: learning to ride a bike.

What happened when you first learned to ride a bike? Perhaps you can remember a moment when you lost speed and were in danger of losing your balance. What did you do? If you were getting the hang of riding, you worked the pedals to gain speed, while you simultaneously attempted to control your handlebars and prevent them from diverting you to the right or the left.

What if you were still nervous and struggling to keep your balance? Probably, you felt the bike moving in one direction and you overcompensated, turning the handlebars in the opposite direction. This overcompensation affected your balance again, so you turned in the opposite direction—perhaps again too far. If you managed to gain speed, regain your balance, and stay on the bike, the moment of crisis was over and you continued on your way. If you fell off, you may have called it quits for the day or gotten back on and tried again.

As a child—or even as an adult—you probably didn't frame learning to ride a bike as a test of resilience. In practice, however, that's exactly what it is. The first test, of course, comes when we must overcome our initial fear of mounting the unfamiliar machine. With a trusted friend or adult holding the bike, most of us pass this test with relative ease. When our supporter lets go, however, we feel a wave of fear as we encounter the possibility of falling off. Continuing to pedal and trust the bike's natural balance allows us to pass the second test.

What happens when we feel the bike wobble beneath us and slip into jerky zigzags? If we succeed in staying calm, or at least in swallowing our panic before it overtakes us, we pass the third test. Finally, there is a fourth test. Sooner or later, we inevitably fall off the bike and must pick ourselves up, pride—and perhaps knees—a little the worse for wear. When we fall yet choose to remount the bike and try again, we pass an even more demanding test of resilience. Despite our embarrassment and possibly physical injury, we take a deep breath and return to pursuing our goals.

Assuming that you have long since learned how to ride a bike, today you most likely ride without thinking twice. Barring an accident that knocks your confidence, the resilience you displayed to master the skill in the first place hardly plays a part in your current thinking. You have new challenges to address.

While your adult challenges are of a different order of magnitude to riding a bike, however, the basic emotions you must confront—fear, anxiety, and uncertainty—are much the same. What happens when you must speak publicly or deliver a key report? How do you approach failures and setbacks? Your decision about whether to give up or try again depends on many different factors, but the subjective experience is quite similar to the experience of any child struggling to learn how to ride a bike.

Let's consider another example: jet pilots who run into difficulties and eject from their aircraft. For pilots, staying in the cockpit and maintaining control is a strong imperative, central to their sense of competence and occupational identity. To a pilot, ejection is an admission of defeat and a traumatic experience: they hand control over to an automatic system, running the risk of injury or death.

Some of the pilots who undergo this experience are so traumatized that they never fly again, while others eventually overcome their fear and return to flying. Squadron Leader DG Fowlie of the Royal Air Force and

Professor Mark Aveline of the University of Leicester studied the outcomes of 153 Royal Airforce officers who survived ejection from their aircraft.[21] The study covered a twelve-year period, during which Royal Air Force pilots experienced 254 ejections, causing fifty-one fatalities (approximately a one-in-five chance of dying). The circumstances of these ejections varied greatly. Some proceeded smoothly, while others took place in complex and difficult scenarios representing a high likelihood of injury or death.

The emotional impact reported by the pilots varied considerably. Slightly more than half said that they experienced no emotional consequences, although the authors admit that this figure may be due to the reluctance of military pilots to admit to stress, fear, or anxiety. In total, 40 percent of pilots who ejected reported intense fear and anxiety that prevented them from returning to flying, at least for a while. Almost all of the pilots eventually returned to flying; only two-thirds, however, piloted aircraft with ejection seats. The others transferred to less hazardous assignments.

Technically, resilience is defined as the ability to bounce back from setbacks or crises. Humans, however, are emotional beings, not technical units. We experience setbacks and crises not simply as packets of data but as episodes that generate fear, anxiety, and anger. Our memories of these emotions influence our future decisions and our perception of risk. Individual resilience is not the absence of these emotions, but the ability to work with them. The kid who gets back on the bike and the pilot who gets back into the cockpit have a lot in common. Both encounter situations that cause them to experience high levels of anxiety, yet they choose to return to the source of their fear and conquer it anew.

To understand more thoroughly how some people manage to remain in the zone of resilient decision-making, let's examine some examples of well-known people who have done just that. You may already have heard of these people; perhaps you have even read their biographies. All of them faced numerous challenges throughout their careers.

---

21   DG Fowlie and Mark O. Aveline, "The Emotional Consequences of Ejection, Rescue, and Rehabilitation in Royal Air Force Aircrew, *The British Journal of Psychiatry*, 146 (1985): 609–613.

Despite those challenges, however, they showed consistently resilient decision-making patterns.

Andy Grove Swallows the Bitter Pill

When Andy Grove immigrated to America in 1956, at the age of twenty, it would have seemed fantastical to think that, forty-one years later, he would be named *Time* magazine's "Man of the Year" for 1997. He received the award for his role in the amazing growth of the power and potential of microprocessors, along with his transformation of Intel from a company known for producing memory chips to a company that mastered mass production of microprocessors—and drove the dawn of the digital era.

Andy Grove served as Intel's CEO from 1987 to 1998, the famous "Intel Inside" years during which Intel became the world's largest producer of microprocessors. He was remarkably honest about how close Intel came to disaster during the transition from memory chips to microprocessors. In his book *Only the Paranoid Survive: How to Exploit the Crisis Points That Challenge Every Company*, Grove describes the numerous crises that repeatedly hit the company during his tenure as "a tsunami." These issues ranged from unexpectedly aggressive moves by rivals to faulty Intel products, including instances of poor management decisions.

The history of business is full of examples of companies that failed to see, or could not handle, challenges that threatened their business. The very nature of such challenges, which by definition require fundamental change, is that there's an enormous temptation for managers to deny the existence of the threat. It takes resilience even to acknowledge that transformational change is needed. Fortunately for Intel, Andy Grove was a CEO who possessed resilience in generous measures. To those who knew him, his resilience did not come as a surprise. It was forged by the ordeals he faced at an early age.

Andy Grove was born András Gróf in September 1936, in Budapest, Hungary. During his early years, he experienced several momentous reactive challenges. While he was still a child, occupying Nazi forces sent him and his father to a labor camp. He survived the Holocaust but contracted scarlet fever, which resulted in a severe ear infection that left him almost deaf. At the conclusion of the Second World War, the Nazi regime in Hungary was replaced by communist rule, a different form of oppression.

In 1956, when Grove was twenty, the Soviet Union brutally crushed a Hungarian revolt. He escaped from the country and moved to the United States to live with his aunt and uncle in the Bronx, New York. Despite his hearing problems and limited command of English, he enrolled in City College and studied chemical engineering.

Grove battled through his challenges and topped his class, then went on to complete a PhD in chemical engineering at the University of California, Berkeley and got a job with Fairchild Semiconductor. Even though his career took off, he was unhappy working at Fairchild. Many successful engineers, both before and after Grove, have concealed their dissatisfaction in favor of the salary and security that comes with a prestigious position at an established company. He had grander ambitions. Grove left his role with Fairchild Semiconductor and, along with two people who later became legendary in Silicon Valley, Robert Noyce and Gordon Moore, helped launch Intel.

Grove might have allowed his partial deafness to slow him down. He did not. Arguably, he used it to learn skills that he later used to face other challenges. In its early years, Intel made its name in the memory chip business and Grove built his reputation in operations—he was responsible for ensuring that products rolled smoothly off the line. He became president of Intel in 1979 and CEO in 1987. During this period, he confronted a challenge that was to define his career at Intel.

Ben Horowitz, co-founder of venture capital firm Andreessen Horowitz, has described Grove as a "wartime CEO." A peacetime CEO, according to Horowitz, leads in times of market growth, while a company has a strong advantage over competitors.[22] A wartime CEO leads in times of danger, when a company faces an existential threat. Andy Grove had already confronted momentous challenges, both as a child in his native Hungary and as a young man arriving in a new country with minimal qualifications and few resources. When Intel confronted

---

22   Herminia Ibarra, "Intel's Andy Grove and the Difference between Good and Bad Fear," *Financial Times*, April 11, 2016.

its existential crisis, he knew that he had what it took to guide the company through this turbulent period because he had overcome far longer odds in the past.

By the 1980s, Intel faced competition from all sides. Cheaper Japanese manufacturers were significantly undercutting Intel's prices, chipping away at the company's market share. Simultaneously, and even more seriously, Intel's reputation for innovation was at an all-time low. Following major investment, Intel had launched its advanced i432 microprocessor—a supposed gamechanger. There was only one problem: the new chip was one-tenth the speed of its competitors and significantly more expensive. What was the company to do? Give up on microprocessors and return to its old products?

Grove understood that making tough choices is part of resilience. Through painstaking analysis, he realized that Intel needed to make a clean break from manufacturing memory chips and adopt a completely new manufacturing technique to successfully manufacture microprocessors. This was a bold move that required the company to abandon its legacy memory business and invest heavily in the uncharted microprocessor landscape. Grove, by then Intel's chairman, recalls the following conversation with Gordon Moore, who was CEO at the time:

> And I asked Gordon, you know, what would happen if somebody took us over? What would the new guy do? To which Gordon said, "You're out of the memory business." Grove chuckled, "He would get rid of us and get out of the memory business."[23]

Andy Grove managed to remain calm despite the existential threat facing Intel. He also grasped how dangerous it was to avoid making difficult decisions. He refocused his cognitive capabilities, exercised the grit to make tough choices, and guided Intel to phenomenal success.

---

23   Laura Sydell, "Digital Pioneer Andrew Grove Led Intel's Shift from Chips to Microprocessors," *Morning Edition*, NPR, March 22, 2016, *https://www.npr. org/2016/03/22/471389537/digital-pioneer-andrew-grove-led-intels-shift-from-chips-to-micr oprocessors?t=1556726044132.*

Arnold Schwarzenegger Dares to Be Different

No doubt you're familiar with the career of Arnold Schwarzenegger. What you may not have considered, however, is that he has risen to the top of not one but three different fields. First, he was a champion bodybuilder, then one of the most successful movie stars in Hollywood, and since then he spent eight years serving as the governor of California—the richest and most populous state in the United States. Schwarzenegger's life is an amazing example of an individual who has actively sought to challenge himself many times, in many ways.[24]

In contrast to Andy Grove, who faced numerous reactive challenges as he responded to the challenges posed by Intel's faltering business, Schwarzenegger displayed a lot of active resilience. He deliberately took on challenges and made choices aimed at addressing those challenges. To identify the roots of this attitude, let's investigate Schwarzenegger's childhood and early life.

Born on July 30, 1947, in a small village in Austria, Schwarzenegger's early life was extremely austere. His father was a policeman who earned only enough to muster a subsistence living. Until the young Schwarzenegger was fourteen, he lived in a house that did not have a telephone, refrigerator, or indoor plumbing.

Schwarzenegger's father was an extremely strict disciplinarian and, willingly or otherwise, the young man soon applied that discipline to his own life. Every morning at 6:00, Arnold woke up, performed his daily chores, then completed a routine of squats, sit-ups, and other exercises. This early discipline and strong work ethic paid off when Arnold met the former Mr. Austria, Kurt Marnul, in 1961. Marnul was impressed with Schwarzenegger's physique and invited the younger man to his gym to train more seriously.

There is no doubt that Schwarzenegger has always worked exceptionally hard. At the heart of his resilience, however, lies a belief in himself and a willingness to break rules. In 1960s Austria, conscription was

---

24   Joseph Lampel and Daniel Ronen, "Arnold Schwarzenegger (A): Strategy or Sheer Willpower?" in *The Strategy Process: Concepts, Contexts, Cases,* 5th ed., ed. Joseph Lampel, Henry Mintzberg, James Brian Quinn, and Sumantra Ghoshal (London: Pearson Education, 2014), 582–586.

mandatory. At the age of eighteen, Schwarzenegger joined the army to undertake his national service. While he was there, he defied authority by going AWOL to attend the Mr. Junior Europe bodybuilding contest in Stuttgart, Germany, which he won. Although this was his first step on the road to a successful bodybuilding career, it was also a serious breach of military discipline. Consequently, Schwarzenegger was sent to military prison for seven days.

In 1968, the young Austrian fulfilled his dream of moving to America and began to compete regularly in bodybuilding events. By 1970, he was crowned Mr. Olympia, a title he would hold until 1975 and subsequently come out of retirement to recapture in 1980. His 1975 victory was the subject of the well-known documentary *Pumping Iron*, in which he describes using humor and other psychological tactics to unsettle his rivals—a highly unusual approach at that time.

When Schwarzenegger decided that he was ready to retire, the natural transition would have been to follow the path of other successful bodybuilders and set up a gym. With such a stellar reputation, he would doubtless have become highly successful. Schwarzenegger, however, turned his back on that well-trodden path and decided to embark on a film career.

Schwarzenegger's first foray into the movies came as early as 1970, in a low-budget movie named *Hercules in New York*. At the time, he was in unknown territory, so he allowed more experienced people to make decisions about the production. When he was told that American audiences would not understand his heavy Austrian accent and it would need to be dubbed, he agreed. Schwarzenegger's name presented another obstacle. He was advised that, to appeal to the audience he wished to reach, he needed to change it.

In *Hercules in New York*, therefore, Arnold Schwarzenegger is billed as Arnold Strong. The man who made a habit of defying conventional wisdom acquiesced to the pressure to conform. It wasn't a successful move. The movie was both a critical and commercial flop. Worse, Schwarzenegger endured ridicule as the bodybuilder with a foreign accent and an impossible last name who fell flat on his face attempting to break into the movie business.

At this point, Schwarzenegger could have given up on his celluloid ambitions. Most people in his position probably would have done exactly that. He decided to forge a different path.

If conventional wisdom held that his bodybuilding, accent, and name were liabilities, he would turn them into assets. Schwarzenegger produced a documentary in which he was the star; a no-holds-barred film about bodybuilding, peppered with humor. The result, *Pumping Iron*, was well received and a hit at the box office. More importantly, it established Schwarzenegger's screen personality.

Schwarzenegger decided against presenting himself as an actor in the conventional sense. Instead, he capitalized on his strong screen presence. When he was invited to appear on talk shows, he was spontaneous, funny, and self-deprecating. The public soon warmed to him. In 1977, Schwarzenegger's social standing was further elevated when he married Maria Shriver, the niece of John F. Kennedy. The match linked him inextricably with an American political dynasty. Nonetheless, he once again defied convention, remaining a Republican even though he was married into one of the most iconic Democratic families.

By the early 1980s, Schwarzenegger was ready to make another attempt at becoming a movie star. In the decade since *Hercules in New York*, he had learned a great deal. He understood that conventional wisdom didn't work for him. On the other hand, he also recognized that being rigidly unconventional is itself a form of convention, which can be equally stifling. Schwarzenegger started his movie career letting others tell him what to do. To develop his star power, he needed to find another path.

In the popular imagination, acting is a form of self-transformation. Actors imagine that they are someone else and behave accordingly. Schwarzenegger realized that he could not perform this feat successfully. Instead, he decided to build on his existing persona by highlighting his strengths and downplaying his weaknesses. To do this, he sought out roles that allowed him to show off his muscular build and engaging personality rather than those that required professional acting skills. In another inversion of the actor's traditional preferences, he also ensured that he had as few speaking lines as possible. By doing this, he minimized the perceived liability of his foreign accent and set the stage for the immortal one-liners that would become his hallmark.

Schwarzenegger tested his new approach in *Conan the Barbarian* and *Conan the Destroyer*, two action fantasy films that gained a cult following. His big break, however, came when he was cast in James Cameron's *The Terminator* in 1984. He speaks only a few lines of dialogue in the movie, and his most extensive speech is only eighteen words long. A large proportion of his lines are slogans and catchphrases, such as "I'll be back." The movie was a massive hit, and Schwarzenegger's ascent to movie stardom was complete. He followed up with more movies in the same genre, several of which—*Commando, The Running Man, Predator, Total Recall*—have become iconic.

This sequence was crowned with the 1991 release of *Terminator 2*. Schwarzenegger had completed the transition from professional bodybuilder to box office goldmine. What did he do? At this point, most actors would have been happy to continue making action movies, capitalizing on their hard-won popularity. Instead of doing this, Schwarzenegger once again played against type.

Being an action hero can be lucrative, but he knew that if he continued in the same mold, he would be typecast. If a couple of his action films flopped, his stock would wane and his movie career could be over. Knowing this, Schwarzenegger diversified into family-oriented movies such as *Batman & Robin, Junior,* and *Kindergarten Cop*. In the process, he courted a new audience and revealed new aspects of his screen persona.

Rising to the pinnacle of the movie business took considerable cognitive and emotional resilience. Schwarzenegger's next move, entering the race to become governor of California, was a challenge of even greater magnitude. While his name recognition was arguably an advantage, he had practically no public record to call on and faced a battle with skeptical media coverage of his campaign. Exacerbating these difficulties, his membership in the Republican Party meant that he could not rely on his wife's connections for assistance. Despite these hurdles, Schwarzenegger beat the incumbent Gray Davis in a special election and later confirmed that his election was no fluke by winning a second term as governor of California.

Catherine the Great Grins and Bears It

Many of us think of royalty as a privileged enclave, overflowing with advantages and resources. Should members of a royal family face challenges, we may assume that they will naturally be able to draw on the resources they need to overcome those challenges. We may even conclude that the royals don't *need* to be resilient, given how readily they can snap their fingers and summon servants to do their bidding.

This perspective, however, ignores the realities of court politics, especially in kingdoms ruled by absolute monarchs, where the court environment can be politically toxic and upsetting the wrong person can be fatal. In such ruthlessly unforgiving environments, danger lurks beneath the glamorous surface. Each member of a royal family must maintain their position while navigating complex power dynamics. Individual challenges to their status may appear trivial, but collectively they drain the cognitive and emotional resources of those who participate in courtly life.

Catherine the Great, who rose from the position of obscure German princess to become the ruler of Russia, the largest country on earth, is a prime example of resilience in the face of constant trivial challenges.

At the age of sixteen, Catherine was married to the grand duke, Peter, who was three years older than her. The sole purpose of their union was to produce an heir. Peter, however, showed no interest in his bride, preferring to play with toy soldiers while Catherine huddled in the corner of the bed, waiting in vain for him to consummate their marriage.

Catherine lived a comfortable life, surrounded by luxury. Yet her position was insecure. She was beset by challenges relating to her status within the court. Her mother-in-law, Empress Elizabeth, harassed her constantly, chastising Catherine for the latter's failure to produce an heir. Catherine endured this abuse with dignity, masking her inner turmoil and impressing upon the empress how devoted she was to her husband. Initially, she didn't speak Russian, so she had no idea what people in the court were saying about her, but she couldn't help but see how her courtiers' attitude toward her reflected the hostility of the empress.

Catherine adopted the strategy of keeping a low profile and maintaining a calm demeanor. This was a smart move, but a difficult one to enact successfully. Elizabeth subjected her to repeated temper tantrums over trivial matters such as her choice of dress. This bullying continued for years, with the empress becoming increasingly impatient for Catherine to produce an heir. In time, the situation came to represent an existential threat to Catherine's position in the court. If she didn't give birth, she risked being sent home or imprisoned in a convent.

Therefore, since her husband was not performing his conjugal duties—indeed, he had ambitions to sideline Catherine and marry one of his mistresses—she decided to solve the problem by taking a lover and conceiving a child. This was a risky move—exposure would have had catastrophic consequences for the young grand duchess—but Catherine was clever and discreet. No questions were asked about the parentage of the baby boy, and Empress Elizabeth—though she knew the truth—had to choose between celebrating the good news and precipitating a scandal. For her own sake, and that of the Romanov dynasty, she chose to recognize the child.

While finding a way to deliver a son and heir was a momentous challenge, the daily reality of petty court politics pressed Catherine very hard. The constant scrutiny she faced, coupled with courtly jostling for power and position, presented Catherine with challenges that were individually trivial but collectively challenging. Catherine rose to these challenges. She made friends who offered her moral and emotional support when things got tough. She converted to the Russian Orthodox religion and adopted an exemplary piety. Whatever doubts members of the church clergy harbored toward her as a foreign Protestant princess gradually dissipated. She also learned to speak Russian fluently, winning the affection of the people.

Slowly and patiently, Catherine developed alliances and gained popularity. Her husband the grand duke, in contrast, responded very differently to his situation. Despite being brought to Russia as a child, he never identified as Russian. Incredibly for a young man earmarked as a future czar, he hated his adopted home. Catherine's background was similar to his, indeed possibly more challenging. As a woman, she was perceived as disposable. Czars had been known to cast their wives aside when it suited them, a perilous position for a woman who was not favored by her husband.

When Peter became czar and started to make his intention to remove and imprison Catherine known, she knew that she had only two options: accept her fate or move against Peter. Although she hadn't set out to depose Peter, she had little choice. Fortunately for her, during her years in court she had won many people over to her side. She had allies in court, enjoyed church support, and was popular with the people. Her bold plot succeeded completely. Catherine took power and reigned for thirty-four years, becoming not only Catherine II, Empress of Russia, but Catherine the Great.

Eddie Davies Keeps Calm and Battles On

You might not have heard of Eddie Davies, but he was a quietly brilliant businessman. In every electric kettle, there's a sensor that switches the kettle off when the water reaches boiling point. Between 1984 and 2006, Eddie Davies was the CEO and managing director of Strix Technology, the company that made 70 percent of these sensors sold around the world. Much like Intel, Strix manufactured a component that few of us give much thought to, but which plays an essential role in the functioning of a technology we all use.

Davies grew Strix from a small British company into a major international player by entering the Chinese consumer market.[25] His strategy followed a path familiar to many other international companies. By setting up a manufacturing facility, which the company did in 1997, Strix developed a close working relationship with companies that produced kettles in China for re-export to developed countries. As the Chinese economy boomed, Eddie Davies turned his attention to the Chinese market. China, after all, is home to the largest number of tea drinkers on the planet. Unfortunately, Strix's success brought trivial challenges unique to the Chinese market that required Davis to display a high level of active resilience.

In Britain, the company's electric kettle controls technology enjoyed strong patent protection. In China, the situation was different. For most

---

25   Joseph Lampel, Marlon Koerner, and Hugh Cameron, "Strix Technology in China" (working paper, Alliance Manchester Business School, University of Manchester, 2017).

of the twentieth century, China had no intellectual property system. Although the country did move to protect intellectual property after liberalizing the economy, the laws were weakly enforced. Local companies had little difficulty copying Strix technology and making it available to domestic kettle producers at much lower prices.

While this didn't represent an imminent existential threat to Strix, it was a nuisance. Mindful of the potential problems if he didn't nip the situation in the bud, Davies decided to confront the problem head-on and take companies that copied Strix technology to court. Unfortunately, in the late 1980s and early 1990s, navigating China's legal system was difficult and confounding, especially for foreign firms. Strix had a strong case, but this was not enough to guarantee victory.

Davies found himself embroiled in a multitude of confusing lawsuits. Some courts ruled in his favor, while others ruled against him. Sometimes regional courts awarded him a judgment, only for that judgment to be overturned in Beijing. Even when he was unambiguously successful in winning a case, the verdict often proved difficult to enforce.

What was he to do? The problem of intellectual property rights was consuming a lot of his time and energy, preventing other aspects of the business from moving forward. The answer came when he decided to turn the poachers into gamekeepers and hire the lawyers who had previously defeated him.

This may seem like an obvious move, but it was actually highly unusual. Like most Western companies in similar scenarios, Strix relied on international lawyers. International law firms represented companies such as Strix globally, meaning that they could promise a single, unified approach with no need to hire different lawyers in different countries. In China, this approach clearly wasn't working. Davies decided that the Chinese lawyers who had faced him in court knew something he didn't, and he engaged them on his behalf.

Eddie Davies was smart. His new lawyers understood the Chinese legal system and the best ways to address Chinese judges. Strix became the first Western company to win an intellectual property case in China and gain effective court injunctions that prevented rivals from violating the company's intellectual property rights.

Were Davies's problems trivial? Individually, these cases were minor. As a CEO, he had many other elements of running a business to handle. Strix's business in China was booming, and it would have been easy to write off the impact of piracy. Davies saw, however, that, if left unchecked, it could become a much greater problem. He knew that he either needed to accept that intellectual piracy would continue to be a thorn in his side, or he needed to address it.

Every person, business, and manager encounters challenges of this ilk. Davies could have shrugged his shoulders and decided that he would never successfully tackle such a tricky situation, in an unfamiliar country, with laws he found confusing. Instead, he drew on his resilience and found a solution. His story is relevant to anyone with entrepreneurial ambitions. If you're setting up a business, you'll encounter many minor challenges, such as applying for permits and complying with regulations. These won't define the success of your business, but they may sap your energy. To surmount them gracefully, you will need plenty of resilience.

Replenishing Emotional and Cognitive Resources

In this chapter, we've highlighted some of the different types of challenges we face as individuals and described the different shapes resilience can take. We've also explored several examples of individuals who have demonstrated remarkable resilience. A common thread running through these examples is the ability of resilient decision-makers to replenish their emotional resources so that they can focus their cognitive capabilities on the challenge at hand.

Andy Grove could have expended a lot of energy railing against the personal and professional challenges life sent his way. That would have reduced his resilience and limited his capacity to respond effectively. Instead of blaming his hearing loss or external market conditions, he focused his cognitive resources on moving forward.

Arnold Schwarzenegger actively tackled momentous challenges, fueling his conviction that he could take on momentous active challenges and succeed even in fields he entered as a misfit and an outsider. He knew that he would encounter setbacks, but with every setback he learned new lessons that brought him closer to achieving his ambitions.

Catherine the Great was thrust into a series of trivial reactive challenges, which she weathered through stoic patience. She found emotional strength through the support of a handful of friends and waited until the time was right before making her move.

Eddie Davies, meanwhile, didn't allow the active trivial challenges of doing business in a new market detract him from his greater goal. He could have given up on tackling the issues he faced or written them off as accounting losses. Instead, he refocused and relied on his creative problem-solving skills to overcome his nagging challenges.

It's important to realize that, when things are going well, we find it easy to assume that we're resilient. We only discover our resilience when we encounter a challenge. You may be lucky enough never to encounter a challenge that tests your resilience to the breaking point. Yet is it truly lucky to avoid challenge when it's in the fires of difficulty that character is truly forged?

Whatever challenges you face, know that, with a resilient mindset, you can engage with challenges, maintain both your emotional and cognitive resources, and find ways to make better decisions.

Key Takeaways from This Chapter

- Throughout our lives, we confront challenges that call for decisions. Addressing these challenges tests our resilience. The question is not whether we succeed uniformly; it is whether we find the courage to bounce back when decisions do not pan out as we hope.

- Our style of decision-making must take account of the different types of challenges we are likely to confront. The burden of decision-making and the consequences of our choices will depend on the magnitude of our challenges. Some will be large and some small. Also, crucially, some we choose, while some are forced on us. They test resilience in different ways, at different times.

- Challenges drain our emotional resources. This in turn can deplete our cognitive resources and make it harder to enact good decisions. Replenishing emotional resources enables us to meet challenges with greater clarity and focus.

- Mistakes and bad decisions are inevitable. Use them as an opportunity to learn and to develop your decision-making capacities. Additionally, use them to gain insight into your resilience. How do you bear up under active challenges as opposed to reactive challenges? How do you perform in the face of momentous challenges compared with trivial challenges?

CHAPTER FOUR

TEAM RESILIENCE

West Side Story is one of the greatest musicals in modern history, but it almost didn't happen. When the project seemed about to fall apart, it was saved by the resilient decision-making of a tightly knit team.

Reflecting on the challenges that beset his team, Leonard Bernstein, who composed the music, later commented:

Everybody told us that *West Side Story* was an impossible project... who wanted to see a show in which the first act's curtain comes down on two dead bodies lying on the stage? That's not a Broadway musical comedy. Then we had the really tough problem of casting it, because the characters had to be able not only to sing but dance, act, and be taken for teenagers. Ultimately, some of the cast were teenagers. Some were twenty-one; some were thirty and looked sixteen. Some were wonderful singers who couldn't dance very well, or vice versa. If they could do both, they couldn't act.[26]

Producing *West Side Story* was an uphill struggle in many respects. The casting problems and the skepticism of the Broadway establishment were compounded by the shaky credentials of the team behind it. Leonard Bernstein was known mostly as a conductor. His previous operetta, *Candide*, had been a box office disaster. The lyricist, Stephen Sondheim,

---

26   Jonathan Cott, "Interview with Leonard Bernstein," *Rolling Stone*, November 29, 1990.

was a young unknown. Jerome Robbins, the choreographer, was highly regarded in his field. Unfortunately, he was still handling the fallout from being forced to testify in front of the House Un-American Activities Committee for alleged Communist sympathies.

Things came to a head as the casting, music, and lyrics neared completion. Columbia Records raised objections about the music. Several of the producers doubted the quality of the show. Money became a problem. The project was short of financial backing and, without the big bucks to finance production, it couldn't go ahead.

Making matters worse were the tensions between members of the creative team. Even at the best of times, managing such tensions is difficult. On a failing production such as *West Side Story*, they were inevitably amplified. Robbins and Sondheim both clashed frequently with Bernstein. Despite these struggles, however, they stayed together, gradually forming a tight working relationship and a close personal bond.

The growing cohesion of the *West Side Story* team, however, was not enough to overcome all the obstacles to production. They needed backers to finance the show and, despite their best efforts, they drummed up very little interest. With no backers, even people who were already committed began to get cold feet. Cheryl Crawford, the show's producer, pulled out. With no producer, there was no show. Everyone who had invested their time and energy into the vision of creating *West Side Story* was despondent. The mood was bleak.

Without financial backing, it looked as though the show would never see the light of day. Sondheim, however, decided to take on the challenge of finding a producer. Previously, Sondheim had contacted Harold Prince, a well-known producer, to ask whether Prince would be interested in producing the show. Prince asked his mentor, George Abbott, for his opinion. Abbott told Prince the project was a disaster in the making and he should stay well away.

With few other options, Sondheim drew on his resilience and made the decision to try once again to persuade Prince of the show's merits. He convinced Prince to travel to New York and meet the team. When he arrived in New York, Prince visited Bernstein's apartment and watched Sondheim and Bernstein sit at the piano, play music from the show, and sing the lyrics. Soon, he was singing along with them. The tunes were so catchy, and their enthusiasm so contagious, that Prince was won over. He agreed to step in as a producer.

The rest, as they say, is history. *West Side Story* opened on Broadway in September 1957. It went on to become one of the most beloved musicals of the twentieth century, consistently featuring toward the top of greatest-ever lists.

West Side Story's phenomenal success is usually attributed to the unique combination of Bernstein's music, Sondheim's lyrics, and Jerome Robbins's choreography. When we consider how close the production came to failure before it was ever produced, however, we must also factor in the resilience of the team that created it and their capacity to make decisions under pressure.

Team resilience is the capacity of a group of people to come together and collectively respond to challenges, whether those challenges are active or reactive, momentous or trivial. The dynamics of team resilience are unique because a team is composed of individuals, some of whom may be more resilient than others. Each team has a resilience of its own, which stems from the manner in which individuals work together. In any team you are part of, therefore, there are three distinct elements: you, other individuals, and the team as a whole.

Analyzing team resilience differs from analyzing individual resilience. When we're part of a team, we respond to other people, and they respond to us. In a team with strong resilience, we draw cognitive and emotional resources from the group. In a team with low levels of resilience, we may feel that our cognitive resources are wasted and our emotional resources are being drained.

Artistic collaborations are notoriously difficult and unstable, which is why they require so much resilience. Producing a musical such as *West Side Story* tests the resilience of its creators to the limit because it requires them to weave together music, lyrics, and choreography. Success depends on each person having the confidence to share their artistic vision with the others, while simultaneously placing their talents in service of the group.

The creators of *West Side Story* combined to make numerous artistic and commercial decisions. The existence and success of the musical stands as testament to the ability of Bernstein, Sondheim, and Robbins to cohere as a team and exercise tremendous resilience.

We All Work in Teams

What does it take to run a great organization? You might imagine that the key is a great leader. Leadership is certainly an important quality—as we'll discuss in the next chapter—but organizations are not run solely by leaders; they are run by teams. Teams form at the very top of an organization and persist throughout.

Does this mean that the secret to a great organization is to create great teams? Perhaps, except that it's extremely difficult to create great teams from scratch. In sports, it appears simple: select the strongest players from different teams and bring them together. This is why "star" athletes often earn so much: because they are seen as a guarantee of success.

In organizations, extrapolating from team performance to individual performance is less straightforward. On a pitch or a court, it's relatively easy to assess individual performance. In a business, it may be difficult to determine which aspects of a team's performance originate with each person. If your role is to assess team performance and select individuals for specific roles, how can you be sure you're making the right decisions? Ultimately, all you can do is judge team performance.

In the case of *West Side Story*, the team assembled itself, which seldom happens in organizations. Like any team, however, the combination of Bernstein, Sondheim, and Robbins faced numerous unexpected challenges. Thanks to their unusually high resilience, *West Side Story* became a runaway hit instead of a fascinating idea for a musical that never left the drawing board.

It would be a mistake, however, to assume that the *West Side Story* team's resilience was simply a combination of its members' individual resilience. Team resilience can grow when a group successfully faces challenges. In the case of Bernstein, Sondheim, and Robbins, they collectively gained resilience throughout the collaboration as they tackled

challenges large and small. As Warren Bennis and Patricia Ward Biederman remarked in their book on what makes for great collabora-
tive teams, "There is nothing like a shared ordeal to build cohesion, as
armies and fraternities have long known."[27]

Ordeals can just as easily have the opposite effect. They can build
resilience, but they can also destroy resilience. Each individual brings
their own cognitive and emotional resources to the team, and the team's
resilience depends on sharing these resources with others. This sharing
is not a one-time action; it is an ongoing, mutual process. In a resilient
team, this can lead to increasingly positive outcomes. In a team that lacks
resilience, it can lead to frustration and destructive behavior.

In the rest of this chapter, we'll explore the subtleties of the three-way
interaction between oneself, other individuals, and the team as a whole.
Let's start by outlining some of the key roles individuals can play within a
team, focusing particularly on what happens when people are focused on
contributing to the success of a team as opposed to the likely outcomes
when one or more people seek to harness the energies of the team for
their own benefit.

Some Teams Are Better than Others

Imagine you have been asked to join a team of people tasked with reviving a failing department in your business. The team has been brought together specifically to accomplish this task; you may know some members
of the team, but none of you have previously worked together.

As you begin this project, what will be your primary concern? You
may focus on the issues that confront you. For example, you may ask
why the business unit is functioning poorly. You may examine the financial situation and discuss your ideas about what can be done to improve
the situation. In the parlance of business strategy experts, this is the
"content" of the strategy that your team will need to develop to tackle
the problems.

Experienced managers, however, understand that the process of
developing the strategy is as important as the strategy itself, and this

---

27   Warren Bennis and Patricia W. Biederman, *Organizing Genius: The Secrets of Creative
     Collaboration* (London: Nicholas Brealey Publishing, 1998).

depends on the team working well together. If the team doesn't cohere effectively, the chances of developing a successful strategy will be very low. In a worst-case scenario, misjudging this step could even lead to the disintegration of the team long before the business turns around.

Any team that confronts a momentous challenge, or for that matter a series of trivial challenges, will encounter highs and lows. Handling the lows and becoming energized by the highs depends on how much resilience that team can draw on. You might imagine that if you look around and see a room full of strong, experienced individuals, they will naturally form a strong team, replete with the cognitive and emotional resources necessary to handle any challenge.

If so, you would be right about the starting point but not about the journey. Resilient individuals have the capacity to form a resilient team, but it's by no means a foregone conclusion. This happy outcome will only come to pass if they share their cognitive and emotional resources with one another.

This leads inexorably to the question of how individuals decide whether to share their cognitive and emotional resources with other members of a team. According to the conservation of resources theory we discussed in chapter 2, there is an inherent tension between protecting and preserving our own resources and sharing them with others. The more we share, the less we have, unless we regain some from other members of the team.

When we share, and our sharing is reciprocated by at least some members of the team, we lay the foundations of a positive spiral of resource accumulation. If our sharing is not reciprocated, and we consequently choose to share fewer cognitive and emotional resources, a negative spiral ensues. In this scenario, each member of the team begins to look out for themselves, as opposed to the interests of the team as a whole. With diminished sharing between members, the team's combined resources remain low. High team resources indicate a team high in resilience. Low team resources indicate that a team is low in resilience. Highly resilient teams function effectively, even in challenging circumstances. Teams with low levels of resilience struggle to tackle challenges and may even disintegrate entirely.

Trust: The Glue That Holds Teams Together

Why would members of a team fail to reciprocate when another member shares resources? In a word, the answer is mistrust. Klodiana Lanaj and her colleagues at the University of Florida have examined how mistrust affects the sharing of resources.[28] In business dealings, mistrust is managed through contracts and the implicit—or explicit—threat of lawsuits. In teams, mistrust is personal and tacit. It is expressed obliquely, if at all.

Mistrust can be a highly corrosive force. As described above, when we mistrust others we refuse to share cognitive and emotional resources with them. This is a problem, but it's not insurmountable. It can be overcome when our mistrust is met with trust. More dangerously, when mistrust spreads throughout a team, members of that team may switch from openness to suspicion and hypervigilance.

In these circumstances, the effective functioning of a team is severely tested. Instead of focusing on the task at hand, team members invest energy attempting to analyze the behavior of their colleagues in the assumption that others have untrustworthy motives.

Lanaj and her colleagues define mistrust as "negative expectations about others' intentions and behavior." When we hold negative beliefs about the intentions of colleagues, we spend our cognitive resources attempting to divine the true motives behind their statements and actions. Our thinking becomes political in the worst sense of the word. This kind of thinking breeds suspicion, which can easily erupt into anger. Both suspicion and anger consume emotional resources.

It's easy to see how mistrust leads to a negative spiral. As both individual and collective cognitive and emotional resources diminish, we withdraw from the team in order to conserve our emotional resources. We need resources for many other aspects of life, so we cannot afford to invest them all in a failing team. When everyone on a team reaches the same conclusion, team resilience melts away.

---

28   Klodiana Lanaj, Peter H. Kim, Joel Koopman, and Fadel K. Matta, "Daily Mistrust: A Resource Perspective and Its Implications for Work and Home," *Personnel Psychology* 71, no. 4 (2018): 1–26.

If this sounds bleak, the good news is that spiraling mistrust is not inevitable. It can be remedied by bringing people together with the intention of achieving shared goals. The key distinction is that personal mistrust can be a function of simple dislike, whereas mistrust in teams stems from the belief that others are not sincere in their stated intentions. We ask ourselves whether other team members truly believe in the team's objectives or whether they are attempting to extract maximum benefits with minimum work. If we conclude the former is true, we decide we can trust them. If the latter, we succumb to mistrust.

Generating Resilience in a New Team

Let's return to the example of the team put together to address a failing department in a company. Imagine that you're attending the first meeting of this team. You look around the table and assess the people with whom you are working. To simplify the analysis, let's divide the team members into two categories: **believers** and **players**. When you conclude that someone believes the team's objectives, you think of them as a believer. When you conclude that they are primarily interested in serving their own interests, you think of them as a player.

Believers ask, "What can I do for the team?" Players ask, "What can the team do for me?" In any team, it's likely that there will be one or two players. They may drain the team's resources without irrevocably damaging its functioning. If players become the norm, however, the status quo may move from sharing resources to withdrawing resources, and the team may collapse.

Whenever a team is infiltrated by players, the team as a whole must bear an additional burden to compensate for those who aren't pulling their weight. Players cost their team emotional and cognitive resources, for example, by starting arguments or undermining others. For a team riddled with players to progress, other people must invest extra emotional energy and expend more cognitive resources.

Even a small number of players who bring forth trivial challenges can undermine a team's resilience. As the number of players rises, team members withdraw their cognitive and emotional resources. What is worse, sometimes believers lose faith and become players, accelerating the negative spiral of team resource depletion.

When challenge hits, believers and players respond differently. Believers look to protect the integrity of the team, while players seek to protect their own rewards. If the balance of power lies with believers, it's likely that the team will right itself, address the challenges, and resume functionality. If the team is infested with players, the team may begin to disintegrate as each person tries to cover their own back.

If you're responsible for managing or leading a team, it's essential to build resilience. Resilience can be the difference between addressing an unexpected challenge robustly and entering a negative spiral in which individuals abandon the collective good of the team and make decisions with only their interests in mind. Building resilience requires you to identify believers early on, *before* a crisis hits, and encourage them to contribute their ideas and emotional resources to the group. It also means being alive to the threat posed by players and taking steps to minimize that threat.

Team resilience is a function of the interactions between individuals and the group. For a team to succeed, each person must see themselves as integral to the team's functioning, and they must feel that they are receiving at least as much from their membership on the team as they contribute.

In the most extreme circumstances, team resilience can represent the difference between life and death. In the next section, we'll examine a case study of team resilience in some of the most challenging circumstances imaginable: when thirty-three Chilean miners suddenly found themselves facing a challenge so momentous that no one had ever survived in comparable circumstances.

Buried Alive: Resilience Belowground

As the example of *West Side Story* illustrated, momentous challenges can galvanize people in a way that trivial challenges don't. This makes them fascinating contexts in which to study team dynamics, especially when a team is hit by a momentous reactive challenge before it's fully formed. For the Chilean miners who became famous worldwide as Los 33, the challenge could not have been more momentous.

On August 5, 2010, approximately seven hundred thousand tons of some of the hardest rock in the world collapsed in a century-old mine in San Jose, Chile. Operational since 1889, the mine featured long sloping tunnels that spiraled to a depth of more than seven hundred meters. The Chilean mining industry is highly accident-prone, with an average of thirty-four deaths per year and countless day-to-day injuries. Prior to the disaster, the mine had already been condemned for its primitive working conditions and poor safety record. Although no one had died, the mine was the site of several incidents. At the time of the disaster, it had recently reopened after an accident involving a geologist in 2008. The miners who worked in these conditions were paid poverty wages, equating to about forty dollars per month.

When the mine collapsed, it buried thirty-three miners at a depth twice the height of the Empire State Building—around six hundred meters. In the entire history of the mining industry, no rescue had ever been attempted at such a depth. Initially, the question was whether the miners had survived. Then it was whether they could be rescued. The prospects were almost unimaginably bleak. But this story is not about darkness, isolation, or death. It's about the extraordinary human capacity for resilient decision-making and the power of a team to sustain the individuals of which it is composed. It's about human survival, ingenuity, and the strength to resist falling into a negative spiral of panic and chaos, even in the most desperate circumstances. The only reason we can tell it at all is that the thirty-three miners—ranging in age from apprentices to veterans—came together as a team and survived sixty-nine days at a depth of six hundred meters. No other miners have ever been trapped so deep for so long and lived to tell the tale.

When the mine collapsed, all thirty-three miners convened and made their way to a fifty-square-meter refuge designated for such situations. They took stock of their situation and discovered that no one was injured. Good news, but hardly a cause for celebration. They still faced the prospect that the whole area—including the walls of their refuge—might collapse. Taking stock of the situation, a fifty-four-year-old shift foreman named Luis Urzua checked the refuge for provisions and equipment. He found two oxygen tanks, some expired medicine, and enough food and water to sustain ten miners for two days.[29]

---

29 Héctor Tobar, "Sixty-Nine Days: The Ordeal of the Chilean Miners," *New Yorker*, July 7, 2014.

The miners were a diverse group, ranging in age from nineteen to older than sixty. Some had worked in the mine for fifty years, while others had only a few months of experience. In Chilean mining culture, the authority of a shift foreman is absolute. However, Luis Urzua had only moved to the San Jose mine about three months before the collapse. He was unfamiliar to most of the miners, and therefore in a weak position to take charge and impose order when the mine collapsed.

Within hours, arguments broke out among the miners. They felt angry, frustrated, and betrayed. Many complained about the lax safety conditions that had led to the disaster. Looking death in the face, the overriding instinct was to survive. In these first few hours, individual miners took decisions aimed at increasing their own chances of surviving the ordeal. Their actions were scattered and uncoordinated. One, a thirty-nine-year-old miner named Mario Sepulveda, wanted to look for an escape route. He found an ally in sixty-three-year-old Mario Gomez. Mario had worked in the mines since the age of twelve, so he knew the layout exceptionally well, along with the risks he and Sepulveda faced if the unstable mine collapsed again. The two of them set out in an effort to locate an escape route and find a way to send signals to rescuers. Other miners engaged in half-hearted attempts to do something productive. One drove a pickup truck up and down the tunnels. Another attempted to climb the rocks and fell off. Others lit fires, hoping the smoke would filter through to rescue workers.

Within a couple of hours, the miners began to feel emotionally drained. Many lay down and went to sleep in an effort to withdraw from the overwhelming reality they were experiencing. This was actually a sensible tactic. When we are emotionally exhausted, sleep is one of the best ways to recover emotional and cognitive resources.

Until this point in the story, each of the miners was fending for himself. They did this because they correctly assumed that their colleagues were doing the same. Initially, it seemed that their mistrust of one another would escalate into a negative spiral. Each individual assumed the worst about the intentions of the others and focused their emotional and cognitive resources on personal survival, even at the expense of the group. The group, some members of which had worked together for years, was at risk of disintegration.

That night, prospects looked bleak. In the morning, however, something unexpected happened. Fifty-four-year-old Jose Henriquez, a veteran miner who was also a preacher, brought the miners together in a collective prayer. After the prayer, Urzua asked the rest of the group to stay close together. In a sign of how far the group had already disintegrated, most of the miners ignored his request and spread out in search of escape.

Day three brought no relief. The miners were still trapped, and they had no way to communicate with the outside world. Once again, Henriquez gathered them in prayer. As they prayed, they began to come together as a team. Following the prayer, they convened to discuss their situation.

Immediately, one horrible reality became clear: they were already running out of food. If they were to survive, they needed to ration their food. This was an important watershed. Admitting to themselves and to each other that they had to ration the food required the miners to make a shift from feeling that they were on their own to accepting the necessity of sharing. Collectively, they decided that each person would be entitled to a small quantity of food every twelve hours, and that Urzua and Sepulveda would guard the food supplies, ensuring that they were shared equitably.

Day four began once again with a collective prayer. The group was beginning to form into a coherent team, with each member taking on useful tasks. Some took responsibility for building tunnels, while others looked for ways to light the tunnel. Bathroom rules emerged and the miners developed daily routines to keep their spirits up. They shared stories, wrote diaries, and sang.

Let's pause for a moment to consider another group of people who faced a momentous challenge: delegates at the Second Continental Congress in Philadelphia. With history at hand and the Declaration of Independence awaiting their signature, many delegates hesitated. By the laws of the time, signing the declaration was tantamount to treason against the British crown. If the war went against them, they would forfeit their freedom, if not their lives.

Benjamin Franklin, mindful of the mood in the room, reminded them that their togetherness would be essential to their success. "You must all hang together," he told the delegates, "or assuredly you shall all hang separately."[30]

When facing a challenge that threatens our very existence, it is natural to think first in terms of self-preservation, even if a rational assessment of the situation counsels that it would be wise to share emotional and cognitive resources with others in the same predicament.

In such situations, individual resilience competes with team resilience. We have a fairly strong understanding of our personal levels of resilience, whereas the potential resilience of a group of strangers is unknown. When we choose to rely on our own resilience, we may withdraw from the group, even when team resilience offers a greater chance of survival.

On the sixth day, the miners heard the sound of a drill above their heads. Initially, they were filled with hope and jubilation. The sound was very faint, however, and their euphoria quickly gave way to doubt and fear. Would the drill reach them? Was it possible to rescue them from such an enormous depth? As they listened to the drill, they asked themselves what they would do if it broke through. This question could have caused mistrust and conflict to resurface. The resilience they had forged in the first five days, however, kept them together.

For four or five days, they heard the drill intermittently, then heard the sound grow faint. They alternated between hope and despair as the prospect of rescue grew, then faded. Throughout this ordeal, they were sustained by their prayers and by the strength of the group. Although they were losing weight and struggling with feelings of disorientation, they found the strength to pull together in solidarity.

The turning point came on day sixteen, when the drill broke through close to the tunnel where they were sitting. They sprayed the drill with orange paint and quickly attached letters to their families. When the drill emerged from the surface, rescuers received the first concrete evidence that the miners were still alive.

By day eighteen, the miners' circumstances were beginning to improve. Rescuers sent them a message and vital supplies: they received

---

30   Walter Isaacson, *Benjamin Franklin: An American Life* (New York: Simon & Schuster, 2003).

liquid nutrition that wouldn't overburden their overtaxed metabolic systems, some basic hygiene kits, and essential medicine. A doctor began to communicate regularly with the miners from the surface, explaining that the rescue mission would take time, and that they would need a daily routine to maintain their optimism. He asked them to perform daily chores and sent down a mini projector so they could watch movies. As the miners settled into the boredom of waiting to be rescued, however, their team spirit began to disintegrate. The humility that had served them so well evaporated, and individuals began to fight.

Once again, the experience of the miners illustrates how difficult it can be to sustain team resilience. In some ways, the miners were over the worst of the ordeal. They had some contact with the surface, and they knew that rescue teams were working on freeing them from their plight. Emotionally, however, they were totally exhausted. Faced with the prospect of rescue, yet simultaneously the prospect of many more days belowground, cracks appeared in their team resilience. Individuals once again began to act with little regard for one another.

At this point, Urzua and Henriquez stepped in. They reemphasized the importance of a daily collective prayer and tasks they could undertake as a team. For example, they were underground during the celebration of Chilean Independence Day. The Chilean government asked them to participate in the event and sent down cameras that they used to broadcast their experiences to a watching world. Being in contact with the surface also enabled them to exchange letters with their families.

This pattern of events continued until approximately seven weeks into the miners' interment. At this stage, fearing that they would never be rescued, many of them once again became disoriented. They lost the cohesiveness that bound them together as a team and began to do as they pleased. Some took to running aimlessly through the tunnels. Once again, however, they succeeded in coming together and reestablishing themselves as a resilient team.

Meanwhile, aboveground, the Chilean government—in collaboration with NASA and the state-owned mining company, Codelco, among others—was putting together a credible rescue plan. Experts from around the world flew to Chile to assist with the mission, and a series of ideas was narrowed down to three possible schemes. Eventually, rescue workers settled on a plan to send a small capsule down through the rock and to raise each miner to the surface one by one. This plan was enacted on October 12, 2010, sixty-nine days after the miners were originally trapped underground.

Although this is the end of the story, there is one final coda that illustrates how the miners had bonded together as a team. The fittest miner was to leave the mine first because he would bear the greatest risk in the case of technical glitches. A struggle ensued because many of the miners wanted to be the *last* to leave, knowing that they would hold the world record for the longest time spent underground by a human being. After some argument, it was agreed that, for the purposes of records, they would deem themselves to have all left the mine at the same time. Their story has since been celebrated in several books and a film, *The 33*.

Hanging Together: Encouraging Resilience in Teams

It's unlikely that you'll ever face a situation as extreme as the one faced by the Chilean miners. Nonetheless, their experience illustrates principles from which we can all learn about resilient decision-making in a group context.

When they were trapped, the miners initially experienced a breakdown of normal working relations. They were overwhelmed by confusion and fear for their lives, which caused them to lose focus. For the miners, this reaction was entirely understandable, but fear and anxiety can afflict groups in far less trying circumstances. Initially, the miners responded to panic by acting out their own fears, depleting their emotional resources, and seeking out solutions and scapegoats. Had they remained in this ill-resourced state, it's likely that they would have perished long before help could find them.

By engaging in the collective practice of a daily prayer, however, and by coming together to discuss leadership, food rationing, and what they would do if they saw a drill, they gave themselves a focus and created a sense of collective identity. This replenished both their individual emotional resources and the emotional resources of the group, which in turn brought struggling individuals back into the fold. Their daily routines, which might seem futile, brought them a sense of comfort and normalcy, which eased the extreme stress of being trapped underground for such an extended period.

Another way in which the miners responded was to become angry. They raged against the mining company, each other, and the futility of their situation. While their anger was completely understandable given the poor safety record of the mine, it was in no way productive. Quite the reverse: it depleted their emotional resources even further and affected their ability to act collectively.

Only when they worked through their initial anger, as individuals and as a team, did they become able to seek out more practical and resourceful responses to their challenges. The strategies above played a vital role in this process: as the miners felt that they were engaging in productive activities, their anger dissipated.

Perhaps most crucially, the miners benefited from strong leadership. For teams to form and evolve, it's essential that strong leaders emerge. In situations where the challenge at hand is both active and momentous, there is usually a clear leadership structure in place that dictates who is responsible for what. In the situation in which the Chilean miners found themselves, there was no clear hierarchy. The shift foreman, Luis Urzua, who would have been the natural choice, was a relative newcomer to the mine who didn't know the rest of the team. He struggled to assert his authority at the start of the crisis, but gradually, with the help of key individuals such as Jose Henriquez and Mario Sepulveda, he guided the group toward coherence and away from panic.

In their fear and rage, there was a risk that the miners would resort to zero-sum thinking, each one believing that whatever others had meant less for themselves. That would have been the response of players. Instead, Urzua and other key figures convinced them that their best hope of survival was to stick together, and that they would all benefit from remaining in solidarity with each other. Strong leadership calmed the situation, helping the miners to retain enough of their emotional resources to engage cognitively with the challenges they faced and to make good decisions that maximized their chances of survival and sanity. By slowing things down, the leadership group created a space in which rationality could establish a foothold and resilience could grow.

When Los 33 entered the mine, they were employees of an organization, each with a job to do. They were not isolated individuals, but neither were they a team facing a life-and-death situation. They were part of a six-hundred-strong workforce. Their resilience grew gradually over the course of almost ten weeks underground. Interestingly, a lot of their behavior served no practical purpose and is hard to interpret except in the context of increasing resilience. With no formal guidance, they understood that becoming a team was incredibly important to their survival.

In business, we all work in teams. As individuals, we may be tasked with developing "strategy content," aimed at solving problems and seeking out new opportunities. As members of a team, however, we must come together and work with other highly capable individuals.

What is the "strategy process" by which individuals effectively contribute their resources to the development of a team on an ongoing reciprocal basis? How do teams avoid descending into negative emotional spirals? As we've shown in this chapter, the principles are quite simple, but that doesn't mean they're easy to enact.

Key Takeaways from This Chapter

- In a modern business environment, we all work in teams. It is common for teams to face all kinds of challenges together: momentous, trivial, active, and reactive.

- Teams consist of three elements: you as an individual, other individuals, and the team as a whole. The team is more than a simple collection of each person's individual resilience. The resilience of an entire team can be greater—or lesser—than the sum of each member's individual resilience.

- Resilient teams share emotional resources and contribute cognitive resources to tackling challenges. In teams that lack resilience, individuals disengage, withdrawing emotional and cognitive resources. When a team enters a negative spiral, it may be unable to function effectively and collapse in the face of challenges.

- Teams usually consist of believers and players. The more prevalent believers are in a team, the more resilient it is likely to be. Believers ask what they can do for the team, whereas players ask what the team can do for them. When managing teams, it's vital to encourage believers and sideline players.

CHAPTER FIVE

RESILIENT LEADERSHIP

O N MAY 13, 1940, THREE DAYS AFTER BECOMING PRIME MINIS-
ter, Winston Churchill rose to address the House of Commons.
After a series of preliminary comments, which dealt with the
formation of a government under his leadership, Churchill turned to
the momentous challenge facing Britain. He described the forthcoming
struggle as "one of the greatest battles in history," and—to dispel any il-
lusions that victory would come easily—he declared, "I would say to the
House, as I said to those who have joined this government: 'I have nothing to offer but blood, toil, tears, and sweat.'"

Churchill continued to speak, telling his colleagues that Britain faced
no choice but to fight until victory, no matter how discouraging the odds.
When he concluded, the House honored him with long, lusty cheers.

The cheers that greeted Churchill's speech came despite the fact that
many in his party doubted his capabilities. These doubts were based on
years of experience of his shifting political allegiances, his capacity for
self-promotion, and his flamboyant style. The new prime minister had
won the approval of Members of Parliament for his oratory, but he could
not command the unconditional support of his party or the political establishment.

In his previous post, as First Lord of the Admiralty, Churchill was
widely held to be partially to blame for a disastrous British incursion into
neutral Norway. On paper the goal of the operation—to prevent German

forces from occupying Norway by getting there first—made strategic sense. In practice, the planning was hasty, and the resulting retreat of British forces formed a humiliating prelude to the greater challenge with which Churchill was now faced. His hold on the leadership was shaky, and he faced a challenge that would require every ounce of his resilience. What would he do?

On May 10, the day Churchill became prime minister, German forces launched their attack on France. Bypassing the Maginot Line—a series of defenses designed to halt an anticipated German offensive—the Germans split the French and British armies, forcing British troops to retreat toward the coast. Surrounded by German forces on land and cut off from Britain by the sea, the British were in a hopeless position. Quite unexpectedly, however, the German Panzers paused, permitting a mass evacuation of 338,000 British and Allied troops.

The Miracle of Dunkirk averted total defeat, but it did not change the fundamental strategic situation. The Nazis were in control of western Europe, while Britain stood alone against them. How would Churchill's government respond?

Cool heads, such as Lord Halifax, were advocating negotiation with Hitler. Halifax had prior experience of negotiating with Hitler and was well aware that the German leader had little respect for agreements. Nevertheless, Halifax, along with many other members of the cabinet, felt that the most sensible way forward was to explore an agreement that concluded hostilities on terms with which Britain could live.

Halifax was in touch with Mussolini, who offered to act as a mediator between Germany and Britain. With Mussolini's offer on the table, Churchill was in a difficult situation. His long-standing opposition to Hitler and the Nazis was well known. The basic facts of the situation, however, were stubborn reminders that principled opposition did not automatically equate to realistic policy.

To make Churchill's task even more difficult, his judgment as a strategic decision-maker was perceived as questionable following the Norway debacle. Aware of his precarious situation, Churchill prevaricated, unwilling to enter negotiations but equally unwilling to openly rule them out. Halifax, meanwhile, pressed his case, asking Churchill to agree to

Mussolini's offer of mediation. Playing for time, Churchill raised objections and conditions without refusing outright.

Over the course of three tense and dramatic days, Churchill's inner cabinet debated whether to take up Mussolini's offer. In the end, Churchill prevailed, not because he made a better argument—objectively speaking, Halifax had facts on his side—but because he succeeded in allaying the fears and doubts of those cabinet members who wanted to fight but who were immobilized by pessimism.

At a moment of great national peril, Churchill found hidden reserves of resilience. He did so not through brilliant strategy or logical argument, but by communicating his strength and determination to his wavering cabinet. In doing so, he provided them with the emotional resources they needed to sharpen their resolve in the face of the coming struggle.

Examining Resilient Leadership

What is a resilient leader? One obvious answer is someone who makes good decisions in the face of setbacks. Someone who can analyze situations and make the right decisions when the stakes are high. Someone who walks the line between rushing into hasty action and becoming paralyzed in the face of challenge. These are all reasonable criteria. In this chapter, however, we wish to argue that resilient leadership is less about the decisions made by the person who leads and more about how they help others make better decisions.

To make strong decisions in the face of challenges, we need several qualities and resources. We may need good information, for example. We may need the cooperation of others who have a stake in the decision. We also need the cognitive and emotional resources to persist, even—especially—when things are not going well. It is when morale is low and the situation seems negative that the resilient decision-making of an inspirational leader becomes crucial. A leader can provide direction, allowing others to focus their attention on issues within their control. A leader can encourage and reassure, enhancing the emotional resources of others in troubled times.

At the opposite end of the spectrum from resilient leaders are people who researchers often refer to as "narcissistic leaders" or, more colloquially, "emotional vampires." These people drain their subordinates of hope and energy.[31] The resilient leader, meanwhile, supports and energizes both colleagues and the organization as a whole.

People who knew and worked with Winston Churchill often remarked on the effect he had on other people. Even when reality was objectively dismal, he energized and motivated them. Churchill himself was aware of this ability, and it matched his beliefs about overcoming seemingly insurmountable challenges. As he famously remarked, "Success consists of going from failure to failure without loss of enthusiasm."

Another defining quality of Churchill's leadership was his ability to resist painting a rosy picture in defiance of the facts, a common flaw in today's business and political leaders. Some leaders believe that accentuating the positive will mute criticism and cheer people up. The problem with that strategy is that people may already know the facts of a situation, sometimes better than the leader. Placing a positive spin on those facts only creates the impression that the leader is out of touch with the needs of the people they lead.

People do not need alternative facts. They need the emotional resources to interpret the facts as problems that can be surmounted, as opposed to impassable obstacles. Resilient leadership comes from providing these resources. This may be done through speeches that speak directly to the doubts and anxieties experienced by listeners, as in the case of Churchill, or through face-to-face interaction that allows the leader to listen and reassure.

The difference between a leader who is willing to listen to and meet the needs of their subordinates and one who refuses to do so can be profound. In his book *Hitler and Churchill: Secrets of Leadership*, Andrew Roberts traces the German strategic blunders that led to the fall of the Third Reich to Hitler's growing intolerance of any kind of disagreement.[32]

The German army was led by an outstanding group of generals. At the outset of the war, Hitler willingly received counsel from his generals.

---

31   Albert J. Bernstein, *Emotional Vampires at Work: Dealing with Bosses and Coworkers Who Drain You Dry* (New York: McGraw-Hill, 2013).

32   Andrew Roberts, *Hitler and Churchill: Secrets of Leadership* (London: Weidenfeld and Nicholson, 2003).

As the conflict progressed, however, he became convinced that he knew best and suppressed dissenting opinions. The worse the situation became, the less willing Hitler became to countenance any perspective other than his own. Surrounded by sycophants, he ruled increasingly by fear.

When Allied forces landed in Normandy, for example, his generals wanted to move Panzer divisions from the Pas-de-Calais to Normandy. To do this, they needed to ask for Hitler's permission. The Führer, however, was asleep, and no one dared to wake him. The hours ticked away. By the time Hitler awoke, it was too late. The Nazis had surrendered the tactical initiative.

Resilient leadership begins with communication, both of salient facts and positive emotions. Resilient leadership also involves ceding power to others, giving them a voice instead of silencing them. This encourages colleagues within the organization to take ownership. When people feel like owners, they act like owners, making decisions in the organization's best interests. Later, we'll discuss this in more depth as we explore how employee ownership, by its very nature, imparts a sense of responsibility and governance to everyone working at an organization.

Effective listening and good communication are two sides of the same coin. In challenging times, people experience a range of negative, unproductive emotions, such as fear and anxiety. These emotions make it harder to apply cognitive resources effectively. Clear communication, the physical presence of a leader, and encouraging people to express their perspective augment one another. In other words, these elements of leadership should be deployed together, not compartmentalized, to build the resilience needed to face challenges.

Howard Lutnick: Resilient Leadership in Devastating Times

While Churchill's leadership resilience during the Second World War is the stuff of legend, he arguably forged that resilience early on in life. As a young officer in India and the Sudan, and as a prisoner of war during the Boer War, Churchill encountered many challenging situations. He also honed his decision-making skills—along with the resilience to bounce back from poor outcomes such as the Norway farrago described above—in various demanding government positions. For many leaders, resilience may lie below the surface until their organizations confront challenges that stretch their emotional and cognitive resources to the limit. One such leader is Howard Lutnick, who faced the momentous challenge of guiding his organization through an existential crisis while battling his own personal crisis.

Lutnick is the CEO of a financial services company named Cantor Fitzgerald. Cantor Fitzgerald's corporate headquarters are in New York City. Indeed, until September 11, 2001, the company was based at the World Trade Center, on floors 101 to 105, a mere two to six floors above the impact zone of the hijacked plane that hit the tower that fateful morning.

In one horrifying day, Cantor Fitzgerald lost 658 employees, amounting to 68 percent of the company's total workforce. Howard Lutnick himself lost his own brother, who was only thirty-six years old. By anyone's standards, the fall of the World Trade Center towers was a momentous challenge, of a kind that most of us have the good fortune never to face. Yet we can learn a lot from Lutnick's response to it.

Prior to 9/11, Lutnick was known as a ruthless competitor, even by the standards of Wall Street. For him, however, 9/11 was pivotal in another way. It took him back to the day his father died, just as he was starting college. His mother had died a few years earlier, when he was only sixteen, and the death of his father left him and his brother orphans. As he recounted in a documentary about the day, "It smelled like, it felt like, it tasted like I was just back there. Wham."

Flooded by the raw, visceral emotions of 9/11, Lutnick found himself transported back to a previous momentous challenge. He had lost his brother. He had lost hundreds and hundreds of colleagues. He had lost the headquarters of his business and—it must have seemed—the business itself. In addition to all of that, he was reliving the trauma of his father's early death. In all probability, he was in a state of shock. He later admitted that all he wanted to do was climb under the covers and hug his family.

But what did he do? Rather than retreat into the safety of his private life and nurse his pain, he decided to bring the remains of his company together. He scheduled a company-wide conference call for 10:00 p.m.

that evening and took a roll-call of attendees. He called out names one by one to determine not only who was on the call but who had survived the attack.

On the conference call, he presented two options to his remaining colleagues. The first was to shut down the firm and attend the funerals of their friends, a path that would likely mean going to twenty funerals a day for the following five weeks. The second was to go back to work, take care of one another, and provide for the families of those who had lost their lives.

Cantor Fitzgerald survived and went on to thrive. Within eight days, Lutnick brought the remaining employees together. On September 19, the company made a pledge: for the following five years, the firm would distribute 25 percent of profits to the families of former employees who had perished in 9/11. In addition, Lutnick promised to pay healthcare and benefits to the families of those 658 former employees for the following decade.

In so doing, Lutnick gave his organization a greater purpose, investing the task of reviving the organization with new meaning. But this journey was not straightforward. It required constant and often very difficult communication. For instance, this promise initially tested Lutnick's leadership resilience even further. Immediately after 9/11, with the company in crisis, he made several decisions aimed at survival. One of these was to temporarily stop paying salaries and benefits. Cantor Fitzgerald was in negative cashflow and, to continue operating, Lutnick needed to hire people to replace those who had perished. If he had paid the families of his deceased employees, the firm would have ceased to exist.

To the bereaved families, however, this looked like a cynical move. First Lutnick promised to provide them with essential support, then he withdrew even basic salaries and benefits. They suspected that he was playing a PR game, trying to look good while his behavior told a different story. Although Lutnick told the families of former Cantor Fitzgerald employees that he would fulfill his promise as soon as the firm could stand the expenditure, many didn't believe him. In addition to the huge stress of grief and sustaining his business, Lutnick received a barrage of negative comments from people he was trying to help.

However, within a few months, Cantor Fitzgerald was stable and Lutnick was able to begin making good on his pledges. As quickly as the end of October 2001, Cantor Fitzgerald had remitted more than $45 million to bereaved families of former employees. By 2006, the company was once again in good shape. In the intervening five years, Cantor Fitzgerald had paid a total of $180 million to the families of people who died that day.

Lutnick also expended enormous amounts of energy writing personal condolences and making telephone calls to the extended families of Cantor Fitzgerald employees who lost their lives in 9/11. He became a pillar of emotional support, not only financial support, to those who were left behind.

Along the way, Lutnick made some extremely tough decisions. One division of Cantor Fitzgerald consisted of eighty-six people prior to 9/11. Only four survived. There was no way he could keep it open, so he shut it down and found work for those people with other firms on Wall Street. Throughout this process, Lutnick sustained a focus on keeping the company alive, bringing it back to profitability, and using the profits to support the families of those who had died.

We're all human, and in momentous situations we naturally experience a flood of emotions that causes us to focus on our immediate situation. Resilience consists of the capacity to recover our composure and take a broader viewpoint. As a person, Howard Lutnick experienced tremendous shock and grief at the appalling losses his organization suffered in the 9/11 attack. As a leader, Lutnick knew that, if it was to have a future, his organization needed his emotional and cognitive resources. He communicated constantly with the people who were going through the same emotional turmoil as he was, with their needs uppermost in his mind. Through this Herculean feat of leadership resilience, he gathered his people, channeled their emotions and energy, and revived Cantor Fitzgerald.

Reflecting on his actions after 9/11, Lutnick framed his actions in light of a personal tragedy he had suffered in his earlier life:

I've been to hell before, on September 12, 1979, when my father was killed. And my extended family, they pulled out instead of coming in. And I was not going to repeat that in my life.[33]

The death of Lutnick's father was clearly a very different experience from a terrorist attack that destroyed his company and killed many of his colleagues. What we can say, however, is that Lutnick learned a great deal about his own resilience from the death of his father. Many leaders who have endured personal tragedies undergo a similar experience. They learn that they can survive an enormous drain on their emotional resources and still find a way to live. When 9/11 occurred, Lutnick was in a better position than most to understand the stresses unleashed by such a horrific attack, and by extension the stresses besetting everyone connected with his company. His resilience enabled him to make positive decisions both in his own life and in his professional life. It enabled him to turn a tragedy into an opportunity for people to come together, find meaning, and rise stronger.

Howard Lutnick's story is an incredible tale of using business for good. Thankfully, it's highly unusual for companies to undergo catastrophic challenges of this kind. It's even rarer for their leaders to rebuild them and, in the process, support the families of former employees. In Lutnick's case, this is especially poignant because he bore no responsibility for the disaster, and therefore no responsibility for making amends. Yet he persisted in his desire to provide financial and emotional support even when the very people he wished to support questioned his motives. He persisted in building the business, even when he was personally devastated and wanted nothing more than just to tend to his own family.

Anne Mulcahy: Walking the Talk on the Front Line

A leader's ability to revive the flagging energies of a failing organization may begin by providing a vision around which employees can unite. A vision is a valuable tool, but it will only be truly successful if it is backed up by the buy-in of those who must enact it.

---

33 Howard Lutnick, "CEO Howard Lutnick Remembers Sept. 11: How His Company Survived After Great Personal Loss," interview by Rachel Martin, *Weekend Edition Sunday*, NPR, September 11, 2016, *https://www.npr.org/2016/09/11/493491879/ceo-howard-lutnick-remembers-sept-11-how-his-company-survived-after-great-person?t=1561737942428.*

Quite often, the actions of a leader don't match the big picture the leader espouses. They may exhibit a tendency to look for quick fixes or easy wins in an effort to demonstrate progress. In doing this, they may solve some problems, but not necessarily the right problems. Plucking this low-hanging fruit may provide short-term benefits, but employees on the front line are usually very aware of a company's true situation. If a leader ignores core challenges, they will know this all too well.

To support a vision, therefore, resilient leaders must take action that reveals their genuine commitment to the vision. One person who did this extremely well was former Xerox CEO Anne Mulcahy.

Anne Mulcahy was a loyal, long-term employee of Xerox. An exceptional salesperson, her niche was in upper-middle management. Mulcahy was an archetypal people person: friendly, dynamic, and good at connecting with people from a range of backgrounds. She was also devoted to Xerox—in the parlance of team resilience, she was undoubtedly a believer.

When the company hit choppy waters, the executive team instigated several strategic moves, restructuring the company on numerous occasions. None of these moves were successful. With the company close to bankruptcy, its leaders reached out to Anne Mulcahy and invited her to become the new CEO of Xerox.

This was a choice that came straight out of left field. Mulcahy was not an especially ambitious person and never expected to become a CEO. She contemplated the offer with considerable reluctance, deciding eventually that she had a responsibility to accept. Mulcahy was deeply committed to the company; in a sense Xerox really was her family. Even her husband worked there. With such deep attachments, she felt that she owed it to the firm to take on the challenge of becoming CEO.

When she took the role, the magnitude of the challenge she confronted was daunting. As she later reflected:

> My biggest fear was that I was sitting on the deck of the *Titanic* and I'd get to drive it to the bottom of the ocean—not exactly a moment to be proud of. Nothing spooked me so much as waking up in the middle of the night and thinking about 96,000 employees and retirees and what would happen if this thing went south.[34]

---

34 Betsy Morris, "The Accidental CEO," *Fortune*, June 23, 2003, 58.

Her first task was to ask people to self-select. She knew that the company was entering a turbulent time, and she needed people who were committed to the cause. Anyone on her team who was nursing doubts would, she knew, become a drain on the organization's collective emotional resources. Therefore, she invited anyone who preferred to leave the company to do so, with no hard feelings, on the basis that it was better to have fewer committed people she could support than a larger number who were liable to drain her emotional resources.

At the time Mulcahy assumed the mantle of CEO in 2001, Xerox faced a perfect storm. In the previous year, the company's stock price had fallen from sixty-five dollars to twenty-seven dollars. Within a couple of days of her appointment, it had dropped to seven dollars. Xerox had $18 billion of debt, with a market capitalization of just $5 billion. Worse, the Securities and Exchange Commission (SEC) was investigating the company for alleged financial irregularities. With the entire finance department under investigation, it was immobilized. Mulcahy couldn't instigate any significant reforms because the department was frozen until further notice.

The main challenge Mulcahy faced was client retention. Xerox's business model depended on providing products and services to large Fortune 500 corporations. If these firms lost confidence in Xerox in light of the firm's possible insolvency, they might defect to other providers, thereby triggering a vicious circle. One high-profile defection could spark another, and another, until Xerox was doomed. Mulcahy handled this challenge by addressing the salespeople directly. She told them to do everything they could to convince major customers to stick with Xerox and to explain that the company was working hard to streamline operations and reduce both costs and prices. She even promised that she would fly across the country to meet key customers in person if necessary.

This approach—combining transparent communication with accessibility—had two profound effects. First, it impressed customers. When Mulcahy showed up to personally assure customers of her willingness to meet their needs, they were more willing to give the company a chance. Second, it galvanized the sales team. By promising that she would personally meet with clients, Mulcahy put herself on the front line, sharing the burden of handling disgruntled clients with her sales team.

For example, she was resolute in her defense of her team, even when she knew that the criticism was justified. When a CEO of a major customer criticized Xerox as slow, inefficient, and complacent, and advised her to "kill Xerox culture," she shot back: "I am the culture. If I can't figure out how to bring the culture with me, then I am the wrong person for the job."[35]

With Mulcahy in their corner even when they faced long odds, her team developed the resilience it needed to persevere when the going got tough. In meetings with customers, Mulcahy presented herself as strong and decisive. She gave the impression that she was someone who dominated her team. Within Xerox, she behaved quite differently. She was always willing to listen. She also encouraged her senior management team to communicate directly with each other as opposed to insisting that she had control of every interaction. By doing this, she created an environment where people shared emotional resources with one another.

When her turn came to communicate, Mulcahy resisted the temptation to sugarcoat Xerox's challenging circumstances. She knew that her people knew the facts. Her role was to provide her team with the emotional resources they needed to believe that they could alter the facts. She later acknowledged that a major part of her role was to give employees the straight scoop on stories they read in the press, while simultaneously giving them confidence that the situation was salvageable.

Aware of her limited knowledge in some areas, Mulcahy readily admitted to the gaps in her understanding and requested the help of other staff members in areas such as finance. She also understood that in times of momentous challenge, leadership is a lonely place. Instead of isolating herself, she drew inspiration and energy from her interactions with fellow Xerox employees. She claimed that she was never happier than when she was milling around with a group of Xerox people.

Mulcahey's approach was successful. Under her leadership, Xerox retained key customers, cut costs and prices, and emerged from the storm. The tactics she employed were not revolutionary, but she was able to generate the full support of an unusually dedicated workforce. Mulcahey won their loyalty, and they in turn did everything they could to support

---

35   Morris, "CEO," 58.

her mission to turn Xerox around. The resilience she brought to the very top of the company played an indispensable role in Xerox's survival.

Employee Ownership: Resilience by Design

So far, we have focused extensively on the decisions of leaders in the face of reactive challenges. However, we can also learn from scenarios in which leaders have deliberately chosen to build resilience into the structure of their company, thereby preparing the organization to address whatever challenges might arise. One such scenario is employee ownership.

When employees of a business own a significant share of the firm's equity (usually more than 25 percent) and have a meaningful stake in the decision-making process, the company can fairly be described as employee-owned. By inviting employees to participate in the decisions that shape the company, employee-owned companies tend to foster a strong sense of commitment and resilience.[36] An excellent example of this approach is Scott Bader, a global chemical company based in the United Kingdom with subsidiaries in France, South Africa, the Middle East, and Croatia, among others, along with sales offices all over the world.

The company is a classic medium-sized business, employing approximately six hundred people and turning over about £250 million annually. From its inception in 1921 until 1951, Scott Bader was a family-owned company. At that time, the incumbent owner, Ernest Bader, came to believe that an employee ownership model would bring benefits to the firm over the long term. Bader wanted the company's workers to unite as a collective and form what he described as a commonwealth. To facilitate this, he transferred all shares in the organization to Scott Bader Commonwealth Ltd., thereby creating a common trusteeship company.

To turn his vision into a reality, Ernest Bader began to alter the company culture as well as its structure. He gave employees more power to make decisions, making managers responsible for supplying the right information as opposed to telling workers precisely what to do. Employees were also encouraged to provide feedback to managers when the company was doing something well or badly.

---

36   Joseph Lampel, Aneesh Banerjee, and Ajay Bhalla, *The Ownership Effect Inquiry: Final Evidence Report*, June 2018, *http://theownershipeffect.co.uk/the-evidence/*.

Running an employee-owned company presents unique challenges. To facilitate discussion and reach consensus, the management and leadership team require skills that managing the average company doesn't require. Engaging all relevant stakeholders can slow down decision-making. Most employee-owned businesses, however, inspire employees to feel a strong sense of ownership and loyalty, which benefits the organization in the long term by generating and implementing better decisions.

Employee-owned companies tend to be oriented toward the long term. Instead of focusing on maximizing short-term profits for shareholders, they're guided by what will serve the company and the employees over the course of decades. This means that they're likely to make decisions with an eye on the future, even when those decisions require short-term sacrifice. In times of crisis, for example, employees may be willing to forgo short-term benefits such as bonuses because they know that the company will take care of them in the longer term.

In most employee-owned companies, equity ownership is a bedrock of the company culture. It gives employees an economic stake in a company's success. This sense of economic ownership, however, is only meaningful if employees feel that their voices are heard in the decision-making process. To be successful, the firm's leaders should nurture a culture of consensus-led decision-making.

Let's examine Woollard and Henry Ltd., a small British engineering company whose leaders have steadily cultivated a strong sense of ownership throughout the organization. The management team is exceptionally open about sharing information, regularly inviting all employees to participate in meetings. These meetings are highly transparent, covering everything from current and future opportunities for the company to the firm's financial position, recent sales, and existing problems.

Woollard and Henry's leaders believe that when people understand the company's overall status, they are more willing to do what's best for the firm as a whole. This provides a number of tangible advantages. For example, the executives at Woollard and Henry have never entered into a salary negotiation with employees. Due to the full financial transparency, employees understand that in good times they will get a fair share of profits. In tough times, meanwhile, their bonuses will be reduced.

Even in businesses that are not employee-owned, it's possible to replicate many of the cultural benefits. By giving employees an opportunity to collaborate in the making of important decisions, any firm can take steps toward generating a greater sense of engagement and agency, which in turn contributes to higher levels of resilience in times of challenge.

One of the problems leaders face as they seek to energize their organization is the desire to balance empowering employees with maintaining their own authority. One way for a leader to empower is by indicating a willingness to listen. If the willingness to listen is not backed up by action, however, it can create cynicism and mistrust. Employees may come to feel that the listening is merely an inexpensive way of placating discontent. When cynicism and mistrust are widespread, employees may withdraw from active engagement with the company, unwilling to expend emotional and cognitive resources by speaking up.

Employee ownership is a way to resolve the excruciating dilemma in which leaders often find themselves: they need to direct their organization but cannot do so without the detailed frontline knowledge that only employees have at their disposal. When employee voice is built into the organization, the insights gleaned by employees are more likely to be made available to top management. The leader can then listen and decide how to act, knowing that their actions will not undermine the willingness of employees to express their views. This builds resilience throughout the organization and makes it easier for leaders to guide the firm through challenges.

Key Takeaways from This Chapter

- Many people believe that leadership requires the leader to make good decisions. This is part of it. Another part, often hidden from sight, is the vital importance of a leader enabling other people in the organization to make good decisions in the face of challenges.

- Leadership entails responsibilities to an organization. A resilient leader possesses the emotional and cognitive resources needed to shoulder these responsibilities.

- When leaders listen to their employees, this gesture can have a powerful impact on the tenor of their organization. Leaders who genuinely listen increase the resilience of their employees. They encourage employees to persist in the face of challenges rather than give up.

- As employee-owned businesses demonstrate, it is possible to build resilience into the fabric of the organization by giving everyone a voice. Even in companies that are not employee-owned, leaders can replicate many of the advantages of employee ownership.

PART THREE

YOUR RESILIENCE

CHAPTER SIX

RESILIENCE IN OUR DAY-TO-DAY LIVES

N 2015, THE SWEDISH ACADEMY AWARDED SVETLANA ALEXIEVICH, A Belarusian writer, the Nobel Prize for literature. It was a notable moment because Alexievich's literary approach is unusual. Unlike most writers, she does not conjure up characters or invent plots. Instead, her writings draw on hundreds of interviews conducted with people who have been caught up in momentous events such as the Second World War, the Soviet war in Afghanistan, and the Chernobyl nuclear disaster.

As the Nobel committee noted in the press release announcing the award, however, Alexievich offers not a "history of events, but a history of emotions." As she interviews people, they relive the choices they made and the struggles they endured in extreme circumstances. Their recollections are not confined to the factual. They are also emotional. These people recollect what they felt during the event in question, and their words during the interviews express how they feel as they reflect on their part in momentous events.

In the context of literature, Alexievich's approach is revolutionary. The biography section of most bookstores contains works dedicated to people of renown and the authors of great accomplishments. This is hardly surprising. Biographers want their books to reach an audience, and most of us are fascinated by individuals who have made history, so it is only natural for biographers to concentrate on the lives of such people.

To some extent, we have done the same in this book. We have used the lives of monarchs, politicians, and great entrepreneurs as a canvas on which to paint a picture of resilience because we anticipate that you will naturally be interested in their accomplishments.

Alexievich's books demonstrate that people from all walks of life can be as resilient as, if not more resilient than, those who capture headlines. Her work reinforces a point we made earlier—that resilience is not the exclusive property of special people. It can be found in all of us, if only we take the time to seek it.

As you have read this book, perhaps you have said to yourself that it's all very well for Milton Hershey, Winston Churchill, or Catherine the Great to discover extraordinary reserves of resilience. They are, after all, exceptional people who achieved exceptional things. Perhaps you have compared yourself with them and found yourself wanting, thinking that you have not built a great business enterprise, stood up to Nazi Germany, or mounted a palace coup to unseat your emotionally distant husband.

It may be true that the challenges you face take place on a smaller scale, in more intimate settings. It may be true that your successes or failures don't inspire headlines or shape the course of world history. But that's no reason to discount them. We all need the resilience to make good decisions when the pressure is on. This chapter is devoted to the question of what resilience looks like at ground level, where most of us live and work.

To examine this reality, we have put together a series of vignettes based on dilemmas faced by managers and entrepreneurs we have come to know. To protect the privacy of these individuals, we have disguised the details as much as possible, although we hope we've maintained the essence of the challenges they confront. By their nature, these scenarios do not possess the emotional intensity so apparent in Alexievich's work, but they represent situations many of us encounter and struggle to navigate on a regular basis. We hope that your own experiences and your capacity for empathy will allow you to put yourself in the shoes of the protagonists.

In this third part of the book, we want to shift the focus to you, our reader, and discuss how these vignettes can help you to develop your own resilient decision-making. Our aim is to highlight the mutually supportive relationship between the emotional and cognitive resources required to sustain resilient decision-making. When all is well, we tend to take this relationship for granted. When we encounter challenges, however, this relationship between emotion and cognition can swiftly deteriorate.

The deterioration is not necessarily a result of facing momentous challenges. A series of trivial challenges can drain our cognitive and emotional resources just as surely as a single momentous one. As we have posited throughout this book, what matters more than the challenges themselves is how we respond to them.

Our work has revealed that certain emotional and cognitive responses to challenges have the effect of transforming what should be a positive relationship between emotional and cognitive resources into a negative one. These threats to resilient decision-making can multiply to the point where they create such a drain on our emotional resources that, to use a colloquial phrase, we "can't think straight."

This drain on our emotions can happen slowly or rapidly. There are no mathematical models that describe the phenomenon or how it affects our thinking. However, we have identified three scenarios in which the drain on our emotions can take place. We call them **mood music**, **chain reaction**, and **flash flood**. In the next section of this chapter, we will provide illustrations of each one.

Mood Music

Sarah wakes to the latest news, which consists of the usual catalogue of scandals and disasters. None of the events touch her directly, but the tone of the information influences her mood for the rest of the day. As she goes about her daily life, she feels a sense of unease and disquiet. The news performs a similar function to music in a horror film. It seems dark and full of foreboding, a warning of negative events to come.

When Sarah arrives at work, she shares an elevator with her superior. He initially fails to greet her, and when he responds to her greeting, she interprets his tone as cool and distant. What should she make of his behavior? Not very much, probably. In all likelihood, he is preoccupied with his own challenges. In Sarah's head, however, the encounter adds to the background hum of anxiety and trepidation that is slowly draining her emotional resources.

Unless Sarah is exceptionally self-aware, she does not notice this small shift. Perhaps it is so much a regular part of her day that she is accustomed to the gradual decrease in her energy throughout the day. Should she take the time to reflect on her situation, however, she may notice that she is finding it difficult to make decisions. She may realize that, with this negative mood music playing in the back of her mind, she has a tendency to postpone making decisions. She may turn to other people for advice, not as a way to tap into their knowledge but as a way to avoid taking responsibility for herself.

You may argue that Sarah needs to look at the events triggering her mood more objectively. If she examined each one, she would no doubt dismiss them as irrelevant or meaningless. This prescription, however, ignores the fact that we process the external world emotionally, and finding the distance to observe our reactions objectively can be highly challenging. Each individual trivial event may drain only a little of our emotional resources, but in combination they can have a significant impact on our moods.

Telling Sarah not to let things bother her, therefore, is unlikely to have the desired effect. It's far more realistic to ask how resilient she is. To what extent can she function while emotionally depleted? Resilient decision-makers can make effective decisions in spite of trivial events that drain their emotional resources. They do this not by aspiring to objectivity or denying the emotional impact of these events but by noticing that their emotional resources have taken a hit and doing what they need to do to replenish those resources.

Chain Reaction

George is obsessed with his forthcoming performance review. It is his first review since he joined the company. His previous company was small and informal, so performance reviews took on a less daunting aspect. They consisted of little more than ticking a few boxes. George's new company is much bigger than his previous one. His colleagues are highly professional, and many of them boast résumés far more impressive than his own.

George received an email informing him of the date and time of his performance review a couple of weeks ago, and since then he has been thinking constantly about his place in the company. How well has he been doing?

In his time with his new company, George has taken on some tough jobs. On the whole, he has done them well. On occasion, however, he has encountered problems that he hasn't immediately been able to handle, and some colleagues have raised questions about his approach. Despite these minor bumps in the road, he has delivered strong work. His doubts going into his review center on the question of whether his efforts will be appreciated. Will he receive plaudits for taking on difficult challenges and attaining some successes, or will he be chided for his failures?

George has ten days before his review. In the meantime, he has a great deal to do. He meets his team to go over a project they are due to begin shortly. He attends a committee to discuss quality standards. He busies himself with daily tasks. No matter how hard he tries to focus his mind, however, his upcoming performance review preys on his mind. Whatever he does, George finds himself looking for clues. What can he expect from the review? Is everyone on his team really on his side? How about his colleagues on the standards committee?

He cannot be sure, and yet he is desperate for certainty. His rapidly approaching performance review has triggered a chain reaction of doubt and suspicion that is draining his emotional resources. George tries to put a stop to this process, but every time he thinks he has managed to control his spiraling anxiety, something happens to spark a new cycle.

All the while, George must continue to function. He has problems to address and decisions to make. Despite his best efforts, however, he is unable to focus on the tasks at hand. He is constantly in a state of heightened alertness. George's cognitive resources are stretched to the limit, while his emotional resources are quickly draining away.

This is where George's resilience level comes into play. You may want to tell George to get a grip on his growing anxiety and stop thinking about his forthcoming performance review. As in Sarah's case, however, this kind of pep talk is of limited value. Resilience requires George to deal with his emotional reality as well as he can, while preparing for his review. In the words of the old adage—which applies to George as much as it did to Catherine the Great—he must grin and bear it.

One big risk is that George may become so emotionally depleted that he will react badly to any negative feedback he receives during his review. Low resilience levels may lead him to avoid engaging his superiors in a meaningful conversation about his performance to date and his hopes for the future or to defend his actions when he would be better to admit to his mistakes. To head these outcomes off at the pass, George must seek out people and activities that bolster his resilience.

Flash Flood

Eduardo is panicking. Moments ago, he was informed that his company's newest product has failed a major field test. The company has already announced the product's release date. Postponement is not an option; it would be an admission of failure. As head of product development, Eduardo is directly responsible for the new product. Any moment now, his phone will ring, and the CEO will be on the line demanding answers. His only option is to call his team for a meeting and ask them to provide the answers he needs to feed up the line.

The meeting goes badly. Eduardo's senior engineer blames production, citing the sloppy fabrication of critical components. Production blames procurement for poor sourcing decisions. No one is sure why the launch announcement was made before field trials were complete. As the meeting concludes, Eduardo ponders his options. Every course of action he considers seems like a poor idea. He keeps looking for a way out of this mess, but none of the options he considers has the desired effect. He works late into the evening, going over files and making phone calls. Instead of answers, he finds only more questions. By the time he gives up and goes home, he is emotionally exhausted.

Like the real thing, an emotional flash flood arrives suddenly, wreaking havoc and confusion. The shock and surprise exact an emotional toll, which makes dealing with the challenge even harder. When we encounter a flash flood, we lose emotional resources suddenly. We immediately find it much harder to make decisions, especially if we cannot see any obvious good options.

Exploring and evaluating solutions to a complex problem is a cognitively demanding process. When the situation is compounded by a lack of emotional resources, the sense of disorientation that results makes decision-making even harder. We may turn away from the difficult process of making decisions, instead pursuing peripheral activities such as looking for reasons why the problems occurred. The lower our emotional resources, the more likely we are to turn to this option.

This is when resilience comes into play. A truly resilient decision-maker postpones the task of finding causes and allocating blame, instead gathering their emotional resources and focusing on the more difficult and painful task at hand. They eschew the desire to seek out emotional comfort and take the first steps toward exploring their options and developing effective solutions.

How Resilient Are You?

In the face of challenges, demands on emotional resources usually engage our attention immediately, followed by demands on cognitive resources. Therefore, the way we deal with our emotions has a significant influence on the cognitive capabilities we bring to the task at hand.

We've crafted four scenarios that represent common challenges. Use your imagination to put yourself in these situations, then think about how you would respond, both emotionally and cognitively. These exercises will prepare you for chapter 7, in which you'll take a quiz to measure your resilience and therefore understand where you need to develop. In light of this information, we'll offer you strategies aimed at helping you to grow your resilience and develop your decision-making abilities.

#1: Isolated by Office Politics

Most of us have experience of people who pull strings in the workplace in order to suit their agenda. These people may leverage a strong social position. For example, they may be close to influential decision-makers. Perhaps they drop names or casually mention attending a dinner party at the house of the CEO. They may be adept at courting the good opinion of superiors yet treat the people they manage with contempt. If you can, you probably ignore these people. This strategy works fine until you find yourself on a team with one or more of them.

Therefore, consider the following situation. Your boss seems to favor one of his subordinates, who is nominally your equal but behaves as though he is your superior. The person in question is excellent at managing how he appears to your boss, and he uses the kudos he gains from this ability to claim more and more authority. Before long, he is reviewing your work, even though his position is no more senior than yours. This has been annoying you for some time, but until now you have let it slide. The true gravity of the situation, however, only comes home to you when you meet someone from another team, who is under the impression that your boss's favorite lieutenant is your line manager. What would you do in this situation? How would you respond?

#2: Attempting to Unite a Disconnected Team

You work as a client director for a leading advertising agency. Your current project is a new digital media campaign for an important client, and you have put in long hours to deliver an outstanding campaign on time and under budget. You've been so focused that you've sacrificed many evenings and weekends to the task over the past couple of months.

Soon after the campaign launches, results begin to come back. The project is a huge hit, and your client is ecstatic. A representative of the firm contacts your CEO and delivers rave reviews of your work. In response, your CEO recognizes your contribution in a monthly town hall meeting. As a reward for your excellence, he asks you to lead a new business unit, with a duty to transform the conventional metrics for measuring success and bring greater transparency to the content creation process.

To do this successfully, you know that you'll require internal buy-in from your colleagues, particularly the company's powerful client directors. You recruit your team, outline your vision in an email to the CEO and other key leaders, and invite them all to attend the first meeting of your new business unit.

As you open the meeting, you are thrilled to be in the room. Before long, however, you notice that the response to your words is lukewarm, at best. Some people are whispering to each other, distracting others from your presentation and affecting your concentration. Although you press on, you face numerous interruptions from people challenging your proposals and questioning your suitability for your new role. As the meeting progresses, you're unable to hide your frustration, and you decide to wrap the meeting before it slips completely out of your control. Feeling low, you ponder your next move. What do you do?

#3: Turned Down for Promotion

People often tell us that one of the hardest challenges they confront in their working lives is asking a superior for promotion. Unlike some of the other scenarios described in this section, requesting promotion is a choice. We don't need to be so direct. We can wait until our efforts are acknowledged. At times, however, we may feel that it is essential to "take the bull by the horns" and seek out the promotion we feel we deserve. If we're successful, we may feel great satisfaction. If not, the response may test our resilience.

Let's say that you've been doing strong work for several months and feel that you deserve a promotion. You gather the courage to schedule a meeting with your boss and lay out your credentials and your performance. Your boss tells you that she will review your case and get back to you. When she does, the decision is negative. She explains that while you have indeed done good work recently, she doesn't think you are ready to take on more responsibility. Admittedly, she accentuates the positive aspects of your contributions to the business. Nonetheless, there's no escaping the reality that you haven't gotten the promotion you requested.

How do you think you would react in this position? Would you feel hurt, angry, or suspicious? Your boss has given you reasons for the rejection. Do you find those reasons convincing? Do you suspect that bias and politics have played a role in the decision? Do you conclude that your position within the company is less secure than you imagined?

The questions people ask in situations like this affect what they do next. Resilience can be found not in completely avoiding the questions that naturally arise in the face of disappointment, but in maintaining a calm, level-headed attitude regarding the decision about what to do next.

What should you do? Thank your boss for her honest opinion and go back to work? Strongly disagree with her assessment? Hand in your resignation? Complain to the HR department? There is no single correct answer to this conundrum. We have seen people pursue all of these options, and several others. Resilience comes from bouncing back following a setback. Which of these decisions represents bouncing back for you?

#4: Unexpectedly Losing a Job

Whether we like our job or not, few of us would relish suddenly losing it. We might suddenly be free to pursue an alternative path, but that freedom is probably outweighed by the crushing anxiety of losing a secure position and the uncertainty that stems from it. Let's think through a scenario in which you find yourself out of a job. As you read, ask yourself how you would respond.

Your boss calls you into his office unexpectedly. From the look on his face, you can tell that the news isn't good. He explains that the company is struggling financially, and your department faces cuts. Unfortunately, he tells you, he can no longer justify funding your role. In short, you no longer have a job.

You wander out of your boss's office in a daze. You were aware that the company had been going through a difficult phase, but you hadn't realized your position was under serious threat. You can't help but wonder how sincere your boss's explanation is. Is he making the decision purely for organizational reasons, or has he been wanting to get rid of you for some time? You wonder whether your performance has been poor and, if so, why no one thought to let you know. Have your colleagues also lost their jobs, or are you the only one facing the axe?

What do you do in this scenario? How do you react to the challenge of suddenly being without a job?

Reflect on Your Resilience

We've shared these example scenarios as a way to catalyze your thinking. Situations like these occur every day in workplaces around the world.

The ability to respond to them in a resilient fashion can be the difference between a failing professional life and a thriving career. There are no single right answers. Instead, there's a spectrum of responses, some of which are likely to be more effective than others. The key is to engage both your emotions and your cognitive resources and to find the most resilient response you can.

Use the situations above as a way of reflecting on your current level of resilience. Imagine what you would do in these situations. They are all fairly common for anyone who works in the world of business, so it should be quite easy to picture yourself in these positions. Then, ask yourself whether your responses are resilient. If they are, what makes them so? If not, what other decisions could you make that would demonstrate greater resilience?

In the following chapters, we'll dive more deeply into these questions. We'll invite you to complete a detailed questionnaire, which you can use to assess your individual, team, and leadership resilience. Once you've answered the questionnaire, you will be better able to see where your strengths and weaknesses lie. When you have a good idea of the areas in which you are most and least resilient, we will present you with some advice to help you grow your resilience, focusing on those areas in which you have the greatest room for improvement. If you fill in the questionnaire faithfully, you can use it as a guide to direct your growth over the course of months and years.

Key Takeaways from This Chapter

- Resilience is not confined to the people we consider exceptional. It can be found in people from all walks of life, not only in those who shape history and make headlines.

- We all experience challenges to our resilience every day, in the form of **mood music, chain reactions**, and **flash floods**. In most situations, our emotional resources are challenged first. This threatens our capacity to engage our cognitive resources.

- Resilient decision-making comes from harnessing our emotions to determine what we value, then using those emotions to inform our decision-making.

- Now is the time to reflect on your own resilience. When have you demonstrated high or low levels of resilience? In what circumstances? How do you think you'd respond to the situations described in our four vignettes?

- It is possible to increase your resilience. In the next two chapters, we'll discuss how you can do that.

CHAPTER SEVEN

KNOWING YOUR RESILIENCE

T HUS FAR, WE'VE USED THIS BOOK AS A PLATFORM TO ADDRESS YOU, our audience. Now, it's your turn to engage directly in an exercise that will give you a sense of your own resilience and how to build it. Socrates famously opined that the unexamined life is not worth living. This iconic statement came when he was on trial for his life. Accused of leading the youth of Athens astray, Socrates stated his firm belief that without self-knowledge, we live our lives forever at the mercy of chance and circumstance. He wished to encourage the youth of Athens to grow beyond their environmental conditioning and become more than passive subjects. For this worthy ambition, he paid the ultimate penalty.

Thankfully, we live in an age where the pursuit of self-knowledge is deemed a worthy objective rather than a seditious one. The principle, however, remains the same: to grow your resilience, you must first understand your existing resilience levels.

In previous chapters, we have provided frameworks for understanding resilience. We've discussed what resilience is and how it manifests as we make individual, team, and leadership decisions. We've used example scenarios to encourage you to reflect on your own resilience. We hope you've done that, putting yourself in the shoes of both famed and ordinary protagonists as you've read. Now we'd like to make the process more explicit with a questionnaire designed to bring your qualities to the surface.

The questionnaire consists of a number of scenarios in which you might find yourself, along with some possible responses. Please read each one carefully and think about how you would most likely respond. Bear in mind that there are no right or wrong answers. We're interested in helping you to form an accurate assessment of your capabilities, not in passing judgment.

Assessing Your Individual Resilience

Scenario IND#1: An Ambiguous Response

Your firm believes in encouraging employees to come up with ideas for new products and technologies. A couple of months ago, you had an idea for a new product, wrote up a proposal, and sent it to the committee with the responsibility of either greenlighting or rejecting potential projects. At the time, you were hopeful yet realistic: the committee has many projects to assess and a limited budget.

When you receive a response, you are surprised and disappointed. The committee simply informs you that your proposal is "vague" and that they need you to be more precise before they can render a verdict. They do not specify which parts of your proposal they consider vague or how they would like you to remedy the vagueness. Baffled, you consider the situation. How are you likely to respond?

IND#1 (a): You read and reread your proposal. The more you read, the more uncertain you become about the project's merits. You start to worry that you were overconfident in submitting it at all.

VERY UNLIKELY	UNLIKELY	NOT SURE	LIKELY	VERY LIKELY
☐	☐	☐	☐	☐

IND#1 (b): You immediately contact each member of the committee and ask them to clarify what they mean when they describe your proposal as "vague."

VERY UNLIKELY	UNLIKELY	NOT SURE	LIKELY	VERY LIKELY
☐	☐	☐	☐	☐

IND#1 (c): You remember that you have previously experienced disagreements with some members of the committee. These disagreements were so minor that you never imagined they would be held against you. Now you realize that you have underestimated the pettiness and vindictiveness of the committee members. You conclude that they are giving you useless feedback as a way to exact revenge.

VERY UNLIKELY	UNLIKELY	NOT SURE	LIKELY	VERY LIKELY
☐	☐	☐	☐	☐

IND#1 (d): You recollect that members of the committee have been attempting to elevate their profile recently. You think that their response may be a way to tell you that they deserve respect and their goodwill shouldn't be taken for granted. You decide to humor their sense of self-importance by making some changes and resubmitting your proposal.

VERY UNLIKELY	UNLIKELY	NOT SURE	LIKELY	VERY LIKELY
☐	☐	☐	☐	☐

Scenario IND#2: Missing Out on a Plum Role

In previous years, your organization has rewarded your hard work, with one promotion following another. When your company's CEO announces his intention to retire, the choice of his successor comes down to you and your counterpart, who works in the firm's other business unit. You feel that you have the more impressive résumé, but your counterpart has been with the company much longer than you. When the time comes to make a decision, the board chooses your competitor. You consider your options. How are you most likely to respond?

IND#2 (a): You think about each member of the board in turn, attempting to figure out who wanted you to become CEO and who wanted your counterpart to attain the role.

VERY UNLIKELY	UNLIKELY	NOT SURE	LIKELY	VERY LIKELY
☐	☐	☐	☐	☐

IND#2 (b): You accept the situation at face value and prepare to do your best work for the new CEO.

VERY UNLIKELY	UNLIKELY	NOT SURE	LIKELY	VERY LIKELY
☐	☐	☐	☐	☐

IND#2 (c): You reflect that up to this point, your rise through the company ranks has been relatively swift. On several occasions, you have secured the new role you desired. Although you're disappointed not to get the CEO position, you decide that staying in your current role isn't a bad thing. You turn your attention to analyzing what you have previously done to attain success so that you can be well prepared for the next opportunity.

VERY UNLIKELY	UNLIKELY	NOT SURE	LIKELY	VERY LIKELY
☐	☐	☐	☐	☐

IND#2 (d): You do not want to wait any longer for the top job. You decide that if you are not going to be a CEO in your current organization, you are nevertheless going to be a CEO elsewhere. You begin to look for new opportunities as CEO at other companies.

VERY UNLIKELY	UNLIKELY	NOT SURE	LIKELY	VERY LIKELY
☐	☐	☐	☐	☐

Scenario IND#3: Handling Unflattering Rumors

Some time ago, your nephew was hired to work at the same firm as you, albeit in another department. Your nephew attained the role without your assistance. Therefore, you're surprised and dismayed when one of your colleagues tells you that other peers have assumed you are responsible for his success. Your colleague mentions that people have been saying your nephew's position would usually go to someone with more experience; therefore, you must have considerable pull. This information disturbs you because you don't want to be accused of nepotism. What do you do?

IND#3 (a): Thinking about what you have learned, you begin to suspect others in the organization. You have had disagreements with some of your colleagues, while others seem to harbor ill feelings against you for reasons you've never fully understood—perhaps due to jealousy over your recent promotion. You find yourself wondering whether they are behind the rumor.

VERY UNLIKELY	UNLIKELY	NOT SURE	LIKELY	VERY LIKELY
☐	☐	☐	☐	☐

IND#3 (b): You discuss the situation with your boss, making sure to set the record straight. After that, you send an email to people within the organization with whom you have and want to maintain a strong working relationship. In the email, you refute the rumors that you lobbied behind the scenes to secure your nephew a job.

VERY UNLIKELY	UNLIKELY	NOT SURE	LIKELY	VERY LIKELY
☐	☐	☐	☐	☐

IND#3 (c): You reason that rumors of this type emerge from time to time. In the past, this might have seriously bothered you, but on this occasion you reflect that perhaps it is better to resist reacting to this kind of rumor-mongering. Nonetheless, you decide to monitor the situation carefully.

VERY UNLIKELY	UNLIKELY	NOT SURE	LIKELY	VERY LIKELY
☐	☐	☐	☐	☐

IND#3 (d): You shrug the rumors off. People can say what they want. You laugh and dismiss the situation as a storm in a teacup.

VERY UNLIKELY	UNLIKELY	NOT SURE	LIKELY	VERY LIKELY
☐	☐	☐	☐	☐

Scenario IND#4: Losing Your Job

Your company has been acquired by a large multinational. Rumor has it that there will soon be layoffs. Sure enough, you are called into your new boss's office in early December and told that your position has been eliminated. Your boss expresses his regrets, and the outplacement team is highly professional, but none of this changes the fact that you will be out of a job in the new year. Rubbing salt into the wound, your deputy has kept his job. How likely is it that you will react in the following ways?

IND#4 (a): You ruminate on the reasons your deputy is being kept on while you are being let go. How did he do it? Did he stab you in the back? Perhaps your old boss told your new boss something negative about you.

VERY UNLIKELY	UNLIKELY	NOT SURE	LIKELY	VERY LIKELY
☐	☐	☐	☐	☐

IND#4 (b): You worry that your résumé is not strong enough to secure a similar role elsewhere. Fearing an extended period of unemployment, you resolve to take whatever job you can get.

VERY UNLIKELY	UNLIKELY	NOT SURE	LIKELY	VERY LIKELY
☐	☐	☐	☐	☐

IND#4 (c): You are shocked and uncertain what you should do. Rather than make a hasty move, you decide to take a much-needed break. In any case, you're confident that recruiting will pick up in the spring, so you decide to wait until then before contacting headhunters.

VERY UNLIKELY	UNLIKELY	NOT SURE	LIKELY	VERY LIKELY
☐	☐	☐	☐	☐

IND#4 (d): You reflect on what has just happened and compare this experience with other setbacks you have previously encountered. You conclude that in the past you have handled challenging situations best when you have focused on the practical, instead of dwelling on potential negative outcomes. You begin by refreshing your LinkedIn page and making lists of people to contact.

VERY UNLIKELY	UNLIKELY	NOT SURE	LIKELY	VERY LIKELY
☐	☐	☐	☐	☐

Interpreting Your Results

Use the following key to tally your answers from this section.

QUESTION	RESPONSE					Multiplier	TOTAL
	Very Unlikely	Unlikely	Not Sure	Likely	Very Likely		
Ind1 (a)	−2 ☐	−1 ☐	0 ☐	1 ☐	2 ☐	x (−1)	
Ind1 (b)	−2 ☐	−1 ☐	0 ☐	1 ☐	2 ☐	x (−1)	
Ind1 (c)	−2 ☐	−1 ☐	0 ☐	1 ☐	2 ☐	x 1	
Ind1 (d)	−2 ☐	−1 ☐	0 ☐	1 ☐	2 ☐	x 1	
						Total Ind1 =	
Ind2 (a)	−2 ☐	−1 ☐	0 ☐	1 ☐	2 ☐	x (−1)	
Ind2 (b)	−2 ☐	−1 ☐	0 ☐	1 ☐	2 ☐	x (−1)	
Ind2 (c)	−2 ☐	−1 ☐	0 ☐	1 ☐	2 ☐	x 1	
Ind2 (d)	−2 ☐	−1 ☐	0 ☐	1 ☐	2 ☐	x 1	
						Total Ind2 =	
Ind3 (a)	−2 ☐	−1 ☐	0 ☐	1 ☐	2 ☐	x (−1)	
Ind3 (b)	−2 ☐	−1 ☐	0 ☐	1 ☐	2 ☐	x (−1)	
Ind3 (c)	−2 ☐	−1 ☐	0 ☐	1 ☐	2 ☐	x 1	
Ind3 (d)	−2 ☐	−1 ☐	0 ☐	1 ☐	2 ☐	x 1	
						Total Ind3 =	
Ind4 (a)	−2 ☐	−1 ☐	0 ☐	1 ☐	2 ☐	x (−1)	
Ind4 (b)	−2 ☐	−1 ☐	0 ☐	1 ☐	2 ☐	x (−1)	
Ind4 (c)	−2 ☐	−1 ☐	0 ☐	1 ☐	2 ☐	x 1	
Ind4 (d)	−2 ☐	−1 ☐	0 ☐	1 ☐	2 ☐	x 1	
						Total Ind4 =	

Calculating Your Team Resilience

Scenario TEAM#1: Disorienting Changes

You work for a major financial services firm. For the past six months, you have been on maternity leave (compassionate leave if you are male). As you prepare to return to work, you receive unwelcome news. Your team is being split. Some members will continue to work in the old building, where you felt at home. Others will be moved to a windowless open office environment in another building.

You are one of those whose position is due to be relocated. You are shocked and angry. You always loved the privacy of your office and prized the spectacular view from your window. What are you likely to do next?

TEAM#1 (a): Talk to your manager and to HR, making it clear that you find the decision unacceptable, especially as it was made while you were on maternity/compassionate leave.

VERY UNLIKELY	UNLIKELY	NOT SURE	LIKELY	VERY LIKELY
☐	☐	☐	☐	☐

TEAM#1 (b): Figure out who is responsible for deciding who moves offices and who stays in the current office. Write to them to demand a reversal of the decision, enabling you to stay in your current office.

VERY UNLIKELY	UNLIKELY	NOT SURE	LIKELY	VERY LIKELY
☐	☐	☐	☐	☐

TEAM#1 (c): Reach out to your new team and arrange an evening meet-up so you can get to know them better.

VERY UNLIKELY	UNLIKELY	NOT SURE	LIKELY	VERY LIKELY
☐	☐	☐	☐	☐

TEAM#1 (d): Accept the change, focus on your clients, and direct your energy toward becoming a productive member of your new team.

VERY UNLIKELY	UNLIKELY	NOT SURE	LIKELY	VERY LIKELY
☐	☐	☐	☐	☐

Scenario TEAM#2: A Lack of Appreciation

You have a strong commitment to alleviating the suffering of children in sub-Saharan Africa, and you have recently joined the board of a highly respected charitable institution. Six months into your appointment, you announce with some pride that an anonymous donor is willing to make a six-figure donation to the charity.

To your surprise, the news is not received with universal enthusiasm. Some members of the board fear that it would be unwise to accept an anonymous donation. They point to examples of other charitable institutions that have accepted anonymous donations, only to later discover that the money came from tainted sources. Overall, the board is split between those with reservations and those who are willing to accept your assurances that the donor is reputable. How likely are you to do each of the following?

TEAM#2 (a): Take offense at the reservations of some board members. You insist that the donor is reputable and warn the board that you will resign if the donation is not accepted on the agreed terms.

VERY UNLIKELY	UNLIKELY	NOT SURE	LIKELY	VERY LIKELY
☐	☐	☐	☐	☐

TEAM#2 (b): Approach a key member of the board, who is skeptical about the donation, and invite him to meet the donor privately.

VERY UNLIKELY	UNLIKELY	NOT SURE	LIKELY	VERY LIKELY
☐	☐	☐	☐	☐

TEAM#2 (c): Table the proposed donation for the present and, instead of attempting to reassure the board, spend time nurturing relationships with members of the team who do not yet know you personally.

VERY UNLIKELY	UNLIKELY	NOT SURE	LIKELY	VERY LIKELY
☐	☐	☐	☐	☐

TEAM#2 (d): Table the proposed donation for the present, and then turn your attention to the process by which the board approves and rejects donations. You feel that the current system is too ad hoc, so you push to update and formalize the process.

VERY UNLIKELY	UNLIKELY	NOT SURE	LIKELY	VERY LIKELY
☐	☐	☐	☐	☐

Scenario TEAM#3: Unruly Team Members

You work in the technology development department of a leading telecom provider. You are also working part-time toward an executive MBA degree. You are particularly looking forward to the MBA team project, in part because it focuses on your industry. Therefore, you spend a lot of time researching the trends that will shape the evolution of your industry over the coming decade. Chris—your team leader—invites you to share your findings.

As you begin to present, Andy—a close colleague of Chris's—interrupts you, making critical comments. Andy then proceeds to recount tales of his recent visit to a mobile summit in Barcelona. The rest of the team seems more interested in Andy's recollections than in your presentation, which bombs. You never make it beyond the third slide. Noticing that you are visibly upset, Chris invites you for coffee and asks you to share your feedback about the meeting. What are you most likely to tell him?

TEAM#3 (a): You open by saying that Andy made some good points, but he hijacked your presentation. You say that he should have waited for you to finish before offering his insights.

VERY UNLIKELY   UNLIKELY   NOT SURE   LIKELY   VERY LIKELY

☐   ☐   ☐   ☐   ☐

TEAM#3 (b): You impress on Chris that it would have been better if Andy shared his personal insights via email, rather than during the presentation.

VERY UNLIKELY   UNLIKELY   NOT SURE   LIKELY   VERY LIKELY

☐   ☐   ☐   ☐   ☐

TEAM#3 (c): You express appreciation for Andy's comments, praising the value of his insights. You note that you will integrate Andy's comments into your MBA report.

VERY UNLIKELY   UNLIKELY   NOT SURE   LIKELY   VERY LIKELY

☐   ☐   ☐   ☐   ☐

TEAM#3 (d): You announce that you'd like to meet with Andy and ask him to collaborate with you on developing the report.

VERY UNLIKELY   UNLIKELY   NOT SURE   LIKELY   VERY LIKELY

☐   ☐   ☐   ☐   ☐

Scenario TEAM#4: Making Tough Choices

It's a frosty December morning. The leadership team of Sporty, Inc., a sports and outdoors retailer, meet to discuss a problem the company faces.

Some months previously, the team recommended the relocation of Sporty's old call center to a new purpose-built facility in Tucson, Arizona. Three months into construction, however, competition arrived. One of the largest wireless phone providers in the United States announced a new seventy-seven-thousand-square-foot center, housing at least nine hundred call center operatives. As a small city of eighteen thousand people, Tucson cannot supply both centers with employees. The CEO of Sporty, Inc., has made it clear that she is extremely disappointed in the team that recommended the new center without conducting due diligence.

In your response to the CEO, how likely are you to recommend that she do the following?

TEAM#4 (a): Demand that the marketing vice president explain how her department got the data so badly wrong.

VERY UNLIKELY	UNLIKELY	NOT SURE	LIKELY	VERY LIKELY
☐	☐	☐	☐	☐

TEAM#4 (b): Accept that the blame lies with external factors that were outside your team's control.

VERY UNLIKELY	UNLIKELY	NOT SURE	LIKELY	VERY LIKELY
☐	☐	☐	☐	☐

TEAM#4 (c): Agree to stop construction and initiate an investigation into what went wrong.

VERY UNLIKELY	UNLIKELY	NOT SURE	LIKELY	VERY LIKELY
☐	☐	☐	☐	☐

TEAM#4 (d): Stop construction, apologize to the board for the center's failure, and chalk it up as a one-off miscalculation.

VERY UNLIKELY	UNLIKELY	NOT SURE	LIKELY	VERY LIKELY
☐	☐	☐	☐	☐

Interpreting Your Results

Use the following key to tally your answers from this section.

QUESTION	Very Unlikely	Unlikely	Not Sure	Likely	Very Likely	Multiplier	TOTAL
			RESPONSE				
Team1 (a)	-2 ☐	-1 ☐	0 ☐	1 ☐	2 ☐	x (-1)	
Team1 (b)	-2 ☐	-1 ☐	0 ☐	1 ☐	2 ☐	x (-1)	
Team1 (c)	-2 ☐	-1 ☐	0 ☐	1 ☐	2 ☐	x 1	
Team1 (d)	-2 ☐	-1 ☐	0 ☐	1 ☐	2 ☐	x 1	
						Total Team1	**=**
Team2 (a)	-2 ☐	-1 ☐	0 ☐	1 ☐	2 ☐	x (-1)	
Team2 (b)	-2 ☐	-1 ☐	0 ☐	1 ☐	2 ☐	x (-1)	
Team2 (c)	-2 ☐	-1 ☐	0 ☐	1 ☐	2 ☐	x 1	
Team2 (d)	-2 ☐	-1 ☐	0 ☐	1 ☐	2 ☐	x 1	
						Total Team2	**=**
Team3 (a)	-2 ☐	-1 ☐	0 ☐	1 ☐	2 ☐	x (-1)	
Team3 (b)	-2 ☐	-1 ☐	0 ☐	1 ☐	2 ☐	x (-1)	
Team3 (c)	-2 ☐	-1 ☐	0 ☐	1 ☐	2 ☐	x 1	
Team3 (d)	-2 ☐	-1 ☐	0 ☐	1 ☐	2 ☐	x 1	
						Total Team3	**=**
Team4 (a)	-2 ☐	-1 ☐	0 ☐	1 ☐	2 ☐	x (-1)	
Team4 (b)	-2 ☐	-1 ☐	0 ☐	1 ☐	2 ☐	x (-1)	
Team4 (c)	-2 ☐	-1 ☐	0 ☐	1 ☐	2 ☐	x 1	
Team4 (d)	-2 ☐	-1 ☐	0 ☐	1 ☐	2 ☐	x 1	
						Total Team4	**=**

Evaluating Your Leadership Resilience

Scenario LEAD#1: Leading an Unpopular Initiative

Last quarter, you gave your employees a pep talk about cost efficiency in a challenging economic climate. In the wake of your talk, Travis, who is relatively new to the team, seems to be on a mission. He has volunteered to reduce waste by leading a "cost cutting" initiative. As part of this initiative, he has proposed charging for beverages, limiting the number of documents that can be printed, and switching off the air conditioning by 5:00 p.m. He also wants to change the company's travel policy so that employees may only fly economy, regardless of flight duration. The rest of the team is up in arms! How likely are you to take each of the following approaches?

LEAD#1 (a): Do nothing. Travis will become very unpopular, but as an organization, we will meet our objectives.

VERY UNLIKELY	UNLIKELY	NOT SURE	LIKELY	VERY LIKELY
☐	☐	☐	☐	☐

LEAD#1 (b): Take Travis aside for a quiet word and ask him to dial it down a notch. If he continues to push, refuse approval for some of his proposed changes.

VERY UNLIKELY	UNLIKELY	NOT SURE	LIKELY	VERY LIKELY
☐	☐	☐	☐	☐

LEAD#1 (c): Lend Travis your support. Play an active role in creating cost-reducing performance targets for every employee.

VERY UNLIKELY	UNLIKELY	NOT SURE	LIKELY	VERY LIKELY
☐	☐	☐	☐	☐

LEAD#1 (d): Explain clearly why the initiative is important to the firm and insist on full transparency regarding everyone's cost-saving targets, including your own.

VERY UNLIKELY	UNLIKELY	NOT SURE	LIKELY	VERY LIKELY
☐	☐	☐	☐	☐

Scenario LEAD#2: Leading against Your Will

You are the VP of a successful sales team, which you have built from scratch. At a social event, you casually asked your CEO whether it's true that a team operating in another region is having difficulties preparing for forthcoming regulatory changes. These changes will transform your industry, so it's essential that your company respond effectively to them.

A few days after you ask, your CEO sends you the following email: "You were right. The team you asked me about is in bad shape! We need you to take over and get them ready. Drop everything and relocate. Someone else can take over your team." How likely are you to do each of the following?

LEAD#2 (a): Decide to guard what you say in the CEO's presence from now on. He is completely unpredictable.

VERY UNLIKELY	UNLIKELY	NOT SURE	LIKELY	VERY LIKELY
☐	☐	☐	☐	☐

LEAD#2 (b): Ask for a significant pay raise that you know the company can't afford, in the hope that the CEO will backtrack.

VERY UNLIKELY	UNLIKELY	NOT SURE	LIKELY	VERY LIKELY
☐	☐	☐	☐	☐

LEAD#2 (c): Offer to take responsibility for both teams, no matter how challenging.

VERY UNLIKELY	UNLIKELY	NOT SURE	LIKELY	VERY LIKELY
☐	☐	☐	☐	☐

LEAD#2 (d): Impress upon the CEO that you don't wish to take responsibility for the new team and offer to resolve the matter differently.

VERY UNLIKELY	UNLIKELY	NOT SURE	LIKELY	VERY LIKELY
☐	☐	☐	☐	☐

Scenario LEAD#3: A Humiliating Email

You pride yourself on leading your fifteen-member team efficiently yet kindly. You take an interest in your employees' lives, inquire about their weekends and holidays, eat lunch with them, and even organize team events.

One Saturday, however, you receive an email from an anonymous account, ridiculing your friendliness toward your staff. The email includes phrases such as "There is so much pressure to do something over the weekend" and "Back off, dude!" When Monday rolls around, you realize that everyone on your team has received the same email. How likely are you to do respond in each of the following ways?

LEAD#3 (a): Give the sender an opportunity to take responsibility for the email. If this does not yield results, work with the IT team to trace the IP address and determine who is the culprit.

VERY UNLIKELY	UNLIKELY	NOT SURE	LIKELY	VERY LIKELY
☐	☐	☐	☐	☐

LEAD#3 (b): Conclude that you are in an impossible position. Rebutting the accusations will open a debate you cannot win, while ignoring them implies that there is some truth to the malicious comments. Decide that the only way out of this dilemma is to look for another role, either inside or outside the firm.

VERY UNLIKELY	UNLIKELY	NOT SURE	LIKELY	VERY LIKELY
☐	☐	☐	☐	☐

LEAD#3 (c): Treat it as a one-off event and take no further action. It's an anonymous email. Perhaps it comes from someone from another team who wishes to disrupt the close-knit relationships of your group.

VERY UNLIKELY	UNLIKELY	NOT SURE	LIKELY	VERY LIKELY
☐	☐	☐	☐	☐

LEAD#3 (d): Address the situation openly, first by soliciting feedback from members of staff you trust, then by opening a conversation with the broader team.

VERY UNLIKELY	UNLIKELY	NOT SURE	LIKELY	VERY LIKELY
☐	☐	☐	☐	☐

Scenario LEAD#4: Blindsided

Over the course of the past year, you have brought together a group of ambitious and creative people to set up your own design studio. You have handpicked your team, trained them, mentored them, and you are on the verge of securing a deal that would take your growing firm to the next level. Unfortunately, today is also the day half the members of your team have blindsided you by revealing their intentions to quit and set up their own studio. Which of these courses of action are you most likely to pursue?

LEAD#4 (a): Decide that they are fundamentally disloyal people and it's better they leave now than later. Cut your losses, delay any outstanding payments as long as possible, and fulfill your minimum contractual exit obligations to these team members.

VERY UNLIKELY	UNLIKELY	NOT SURE	LIKELY	VERY LIKELY
☐	☐	☐	☐	☐

LEAD#4 (b): Suspect that there is a ringleader who is responsible for this plan. Identify the ringleader, and make that person an offer they can't refuse.

VERY UNLIKELY	UNLIKELY	NOT SURE	LIKELY	VERY LIKELY
☐	☐	☐	☐	☐

LEAD#4 (c): Talk to each employee individually, share your vision for the firm, and impress on each one the part he or she can play in realizing that vision.

VERY UNLIKELY	UNLIKELY	NOT SURE	LIKELY	VERY LIKELY
☐	☐	☐	☐	☐

LEAD#4 (d): Offer them more ownership and voice in the company. Give them an opportunity to purchase equity in the company and allow them a greater role in decision-making. Frame your proposal as a chance to set up their own studio within the existing company.

VERY UNLIKELY	UNLIKELY	NOT SURE	LIKELY	VERY LIKELY
☐	☐	☐	☐	☐

Interpreting Your Results

Use the following key to tally your answers from this section.

QUESTION	Very Unlikely	Unlikely	Not Sure	Likely	Very Likely	Multiplier	TOTAL
			RESPONSE				
Lead1 (a)	–2 ☐	–1 ☐	0 ☐	1 ☐	2 ☐	x (–1)	
Lead1 (b)	–2 ☐	–1 ☐	0 ☐	1 ☐	2 ☐	x (–1)	
Lead1 (c)	–2 ☐	–1 ☐	0 ☐	1 ☐	2 ☐	x 1	
Lead1 (d)	–2 ☐	–1 ☐	0 ☐	1 ☐	2 ☐	x 1	
						Total Lead1	=
Lead2 (a)	–2 ☐	–1 ☐	0 ☐	1 ☐	2 ☐	x (–1)	
Lead2 (b)	–2 ☐	–1 ☐	0 ☐	1 ☐	2 ☐	x (–1)	
Lead2 (c)	–2 ☐	–1 ☐	0 ☐	1 ☐	2 ☐	x 1	
Lead2 (d)	–2 ☐	–1 ☐	0 ☐	1 ☐	2 ☐	x 1	
						Total Lead2	=
Lead3 (a)	–2 ☐	–1 ☐	0 ☐	1 ☐	2 ☐	x (–1)	
Lead3 (b)	–2 ☐	–1 ☐	0 ☐	1 ☐	2 ☐	x (–1)	
Lead3 (c)	–2 ☐	–1 ☐	0 ☐	1 ☐	2 ☐	x 1	
Lead3 (d)	–2 ☐	–1 ☐	0 ☐	1 ☐	2 ☐	x 1	
						Total Lead3	=
Lead4 (a)	–2 ☐	–1 ☐	0 ☐	1 ☐	2 ☐	x (–1)	
Lead4 (b)	–2 ☐	–1 ☐	0 ☐	1 ☐	2 ☐	x (–1)	
Lead4 (c)	–2 ☐	–1 ☐	0 ☐	1 ☐	2 ☐	x 1	
Lead4 (d)	–2 ☐	–1 ☐	0 ☐	1 ☐	2 ☐	x 1	
						Total Lead4	=

Map Your Resilience Reserves

When you've filled in each answer key, map the results onto this table. Shade in each column with your score for the relevant type of resilience. When you've done this, you'll be able to see at a glance the areas in which you're strongest and those in which you have work to do.

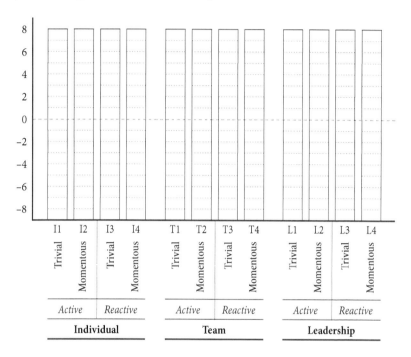

Using Your Results to Grow Your Individual Resilience

Now that you've completed the questionnaire and built a map of your resilience, you should have a sense of the types of situations in which you're likely to thrive and the types of situations in which you're liable to struggle. You should be developing a clear picture of where you're strongest and where you have scope for improvement. With this information, we can provide you with guidance about how to maximize your resilience and address the areas in which you would like to grow your resilient decision-making capabilities.

Before you turn this page, make sure you have your scores for individual resilience, team resilience, and leadership resilience. Now that you've undertaken this exercise, the next step is to apply your results to the task of growing your resilience.

Growing your resilience is an ongoing process. The author and science journalist Daniel Goleman maintains that "Resilience is a skill that you can develop over time with practice. It is like a muscle."[37] As with exercise, there is no fixed end point at which you will be able to confidently declare that you have arrived. In life, we are always learning—that's what makes it interesting. Nonetheless, we can certainly improve, gaining greater skills and deeper satisfaction. In the following chapter, we'll break down what you need to do to raise negative scores and what you should remain focused on to sustain—and continue to improve—positive scores.

---

37   Daniel Goleman (@DanielGolemanEI), "Resilience is a skill that you develop over time with practice. It is like a muscle," Twitter, October 4, 2017, 12:20 p.m., *https://twitter.com/danielgolemanei/status/915657810586800128.*

Key Takeaways from This Chapter

- Socrates said that the unexamined life is not worth living. His passionate defense of self-awareness cost him his life. Nowadays, we all need to be self-aware to deal with challenges. Before we can grow our resilience, we must understand our current strengths and weaknesses.

- The questionnaire in this chapter will help you to build a map of your existing capacities. As you consider your likely responses, you will discover areas in which you are more resilient than others. This insight is invaluable.

- Tally up your results using the answer key, and keep them with you as you read through the following chapter. In it, you will discover strategies you can put into practice to grow your resilience.

- Remember that you will get much more out of this book if you engage with the exercises than you will if you read it passively. We aim to give you tools that you can use to increase your resilience. They will only work if you use them.

- Developing resilience is a journey that has no final destination. There is always room for further growth and development.

CHAPTER EIGHT

GROWING YOUR RESILIENCE

S ELF-AWARENESS IS AN EXCELLENT FIRST STEP. HOWEVER, UNTIL self-awareness is paired with action, only half the battle is won. To make the most of the insights you have gleaned from completing the questionnaire in the previous chapter and mapping your resilience, you will need to do the things that help you to increase your levels of resilience, particularly in the areas in which you have discovered a weakness.

In this chapter, we will provide you with recommendations that you can use to grow your individual, team, and leadership resilience. While some are consistent in different categories, others differ. To use them effectively, find a way of working them into your daily life. You may wish to post reminders on your fridge door or connect with a friend or colleague and keep one another accountable.

Another good move is to keep notes on your progress. Unless you do this, you may find it difficult to make an accurate comparison when you try to recall your development over a month, a year, or a decade. When you encounter a challenging situation, it's highly motivating to look back into the past and realize that you are responding with much more resilience than you did the last time you experienced a similar scenario. Revisit the questionnaire and your answers every few months and assess your growth.

Without further ado, allow us to present our recommendations. Here's to your resilience.

Recommendations
for Growing Your Individual Resilience

Individual Resilience: Momentous Active

If your score in this area is below zero, you probably find it difficult to accept disappointment. A resilient response to disappointments requires you to walk the line between accepting disappointments for what they are and finding a resourceful next move. The risk is that you will allow resentment to dictate your attitude, possibly with worse consequences than the original setback. Consider these strategies:

- Sit with your emotions before you contemplate your next move. This is not a time for impulsiveness. Fully assess what your emotions are telling you before you come to a decision about what to do next. Remember that the key is to engage your emotional resources and your cognitive resources in tandem.

- Develop the ability to distinguish between obstacles you can overcome and those that are beyond your power to overcome. Don't spend your precious emotional and cognitive resources on challenges that you know will not yield to your efforts. Focus on those scenarios in which you can make progress.

If your score in this section is greater than zero, it's likely that you're inclined to swiftly put disappointments behind you and move on. You're relatively resilient when confronting bad news and taking constructive action. To build your resilience further, explore the following:

- Investigate the balance between diagnosing problems and taking action. While it's important to handle momentous active challenges constructively, it's important to fully engage your emotions. Action orientation can be a way to bypass the pain of confronting a difficulty. Do you ever act decisively in an effort to feel strong, before you have truly settled on a constructive plan? If so, be aware of this tendency and work to ensure that you pause before leaping into action.

Individual Resilience: Momentous Reactive

If your score in this area is below zero, you probably doubt your ability to cope with the type of major events that may unexpectedly upend your life. While this is understandable—momentous reactive challenges are perhaps the most daunting that you'll encounter—you can restore your resilience by taking a deep breath and finding a sense of perspective. Remember that people lose their jobs and go through other major challenges all the time. This needn't be a precursor to despair. Whatever situation you're in, or could be in, don't allow it to undermine your sense of self-efficacy.

To grow your capacity to respond resiliently to unexpected events with momentous consequences, consider the following:

- Yes, some events are outside your control. This doesn't mean that *all* events are outside your control. You can bolster your resilience by focusing on the elements of the situation that you *can* shape, in spite of the obstacles. To remind yourself of your capacities, reflect on past occasions where you found a measure of control in seemingly chaotic situations.

- When you confront events that are outside your control, it is natural to seek out explanations. Nonetheless, obsessively looking for explanations when you only have fragments of information is destructive. Stay focused on what you know, and avoid falling into the trap of endless speculation. Uninformed guesswork will only lead you toward anger or depression. If you find it difficult to counter this negative spiral, request feedback from trusted friends. Often, ideas that seem plausible in your head lose their power when you speak them aloud.

If your score is higher than zero, you probably feel relatively comfortable in momentous reactive scenarios. Perhaps you've already experienced a similar situation, so you know that you can cope if necessary. To develop your resilience in this further, try this:

- Recall a momentous challenge you've dealt with previously. Reflect on how you dealt with it. What did you do well? What did you do badly? How could you improve in a similar situation?

Individual Resilience: Trivial Active

If you scored less than zero in this section of the questionnaire, you probably allocate the trivial challenges with which you choose to engage more energy than they deserve. Trivial challenges often emerge when we have developed the basic framework of a project and are working toward our goals. Addressing these challenges may consume vital emotional and cognitive resources that we need to pursue our goals. To grow your resilience in situations where trivial challenges emerge, consider the following:

- Trivial challenges often generate frustration. Frustration consumes emotional resources and can make goals seem more distant than they previously appeared. Excessive trivial challenges can crowd our vision, causing us to conclude that goals are unachievable. Make a list of your trivial challenges so that you can put them into perspective.

- Be patient with your trivial challenges. They can easily mount up, affecting your mood and draining your resources. If you're unsure how patient you are, ask trusted friends, colleagues, or your partner. You may be surprised by what you learn.

If your score in this section is greater than zero, you clearly have the resilience to deal with most active trivial challenges. The question is whether those trivial challenges are essential to your larger goals. One of your authors, Joseph, has a dog named Freddy. Every time Freddy catches a glimpse of the cat next door, he rushes all over the garden, barking maniacally. In practical terms, catching that cat will not change Freddy's life, yet he treats it as though it were the quest for the holy grail. To assess your approach to active trivial challenges:

- Consider whether you tend to address trivial challenges simply because you can. Do you tend to escalate your commitment to goals that feel easily achievable as opposed to those that are mission critical? If so, take a step back and ask yourself what is most important to you. Then focus your energies on those objectives.

Individual Resilience: Trivial Reactive

If your score in this area is less than zero, you may find that you are easily thrown off balance by trivial incidents. We all operate within a comfort zone most of the time. Trivial incidents that threaten our safety may lead us to take unnecessary actions with negative consequences. To increase your resilience in the trivial situations you encounter, consider the following:

- Avoid the tendency to catastrophize minor incidents by overstating their significance. This means resisting the urge to respond right away to situations that don't require a response. Choose to focus your attention on something else while you allow your mind to work in the background. Taking a cooling-off period will increase your resilience and make it more likely that you will make strong decisions at the appropriate time.

- Understand the difference between inaction in the face of momentous challenges, which is often an indication of threat rigidity, and inaction in the face of trivial challenges, which is often an indication that you have a solid grasp of your priorities.

If your score is greater than zero, you clearly have a degree of resilience when dealing with trivial challenges. You're not unduly bothered by minor issues or provoked into premature action. To foster your resilience further, consider the following:

- Resilience in the face of trivial challenges is easily confused with avoidance behavior. To assess whether you're succumbing to the latter, ask yourself whether you tend not to want to know about unpleasant trivial issues. If you are aware but undistracted, that's resilience.

If you sometimes ignore minor issues that nonetheless require your attention, you have work to do on building your resilience. Aim to confront and resolve trivial challenges, not merely avoid them.

Growing Your Team Resilience

Team Resilience: Momentous Active

If your score for this section of the questionnaire is low, your task is to evaluate and improve the way your team responds to unpredictable future trajectories. While actively pursuing momentous challenges, can you count on team members who are full of ideas and enthusiasm? Are your team members willing to adapt to changing circumstances? Alternatively, are your team members resistant to change? How is positivity and solution orientation perceived among your team?

To boost your team's resilience in this area, consider the following strategies:

- Ask yourself whether every member of your team is contributing actively. If some aren't, why not? Assess whether there is a status imbalance among team members. For example, do powerful team members wield influence using cliques? Are particular types of work celebrated or criticized disproportionately?

- Look at your team's objectives. How strongly do people identify with those objectives? If your team isn't pursuing clearly stated objectives, does it operate well without them, or would it work better with them? What objectives would people rally around? Can you work with others to set such objectives?

- Make the most of occasions when the team meets informally (e.g., off-site) to encourage a sense of common purpose, directing the energy of members toward shared, agreed-upon goals. Be willing to give other team members compliments. Highlight how each person's work contributes to the organization's overall goals.

- Champion a code of practice regarding team processes. What expectations can everyone cohere around? How are new ideas selected? How are quieter members of the group encouraged to share their insights?

If your score is positive, you probably know what it is to be part of a team that has a clear sense of direction and galvanizes its members to actively pursue momentous challenges. To preserve your team's resilience, try the following:

- Make sure that you understand the factors that bond your team together. Do they value the norms, practices, reward systems, or other elements of your organizational culture? Actively pursuing momentous challenges requires a lot of energy. Ask yourself how you can preserve and replenish the energy of your team.

Team Resilience: Momentous Reactive

If you scored less than zero for the momentous reactive section of the questionnaire, consider how your team responds to unexpected challenges. How does your team regard itself when the pressure is on? Do people behave as though they are under siege? Do they become paralyzed? Do individuals knowingly or unknowingly heighten the uncertainty in the team by spreading panic?

To grow your team's resilience for unexpected events with momentous consequences for your team, try these strategies:

- Encourage members of your team to resist the urge to locate responsibility for the unfolding situation on events outside their control.

- Equally, discourage team members from making snap judgments based on partial information.

- To aid this process, work with others on your team to slow down the process of responding to challenges. Initially, work with other team members to focus efforts toward developing a fuller picture of the challenge. Think diagnosis before cure.

- Foster a sense of team morale and work actively to support positive attitudes throughout the momentous challenge. Injecting lightness into team environments during momentous challenges helps teams build cohesion and makes it easier for leaders to manage a diverse flow of ideas.

- Encourage debate on the worst-case scenario so that team members feel their fears are openly addressed. Also discuss a best-case scenario to sustain positivity and motivation.

If your score is greater than zero, you have some belief in your team to respond to momentous events. To preserve or further strengthen your team's resilience, you can:

- Keep a close eye on what team members value the most and aim to meet those values. Only when you know what team members truly value will you be able to support the formation of a strong team identity and mutually reinforce culture, especially during challenging times.

Team Resilience: Trivial Active

If your score for the trivial active section of our questionnaire is less than zero, pay close attention to the strategies your team uses to actively pursue trivial challenges. For example, what steps, if any, do you take to compensate for the loss of a team member whose positive attitude cheered people up during difficult times? What role will you play in sustaining team spirit? What would you look for in a replacement? Scenarios like this represent opportunities to actively develop your role in boosting your team's resilience when facing trivial challenges.

To grow your team's resilience in this area, consider the following:

- Take this opportunity to think about your team's work. Does the team have formal objectives? Is everyone on the team aware of these objectives? Compared to other members of the team, are you more or less invested in these objectives?

- Pay attention to the emotional culture of your team. Play your part in encouraging emotional honesty. For example, you can engage in friendly "water cooler" conversations. These will help break down barriers between team members, encourage transparency, and facilitate a free flow of information.

- Double down on practices that nurture believers and dissuade players. This can be both positive, such as rewarding the behavior you wish to encourage, and preventative, such as rotating team leadership (if possible). Work to ensure no one uses their position to exercise undue influence.

If your score is positive, it appears that you are part of a team in which individual members feel comfortable pursuing trivial challenges. Ideally, this is because they feel that their knowledge is valuable, and they are trusted to make their own decisions. To maintain and grow this dynamic, you can:

- Encourage team members to understand the distinction between trivial and momentous challenges. Look for ways to guard against the team spending excessive time on minor achievements at the expense of its core responsibilities.

Team Resilience: Trivial Reactive

If your score in the trivial reactive section of the questionnaire is low, evaluate how members of your team respond to trivial challenges such as tension in the office or insensitive remarks made by one team member to another. While these may seem like minor matters, allowing them to fester may damage your team's performance and ability to make good decisions.

To help your team grow its resilience in the face of trivial reactive challenges, consider the following:

- Take a moment to pause and recognize the distinction between the trivial and the momentous. Once you've identified the trivial challenges you want to address, aim to set aside time for unstructured conversation with other members of the team, with the goal of encouraging awareness about the impact of trivial challenges and agreeing on solutions. During the discussion, support people in airing their concerns in public as well as private. Find ways to make it easier for them to do so. You may wish to express your disapproval of the damage caused by ill-informed gossip and reinforce the value of transparent communication.

- Assess and monitor your team's emotional resources. How easily are they depleted? Encourage and support processes that give team members an opportunity to feel heard and understood.

If your score is greater than zero, you probably have some experience with being part of a team in which members' sense of higher purpose prevents the team's energy from being diverted to marginal events. To reinforce the robustness of your team, you may need to:

- Uphold the distinction between the important and the trivial. We all have limited energy, and it's important that we use it effectively. This is especially true when the team is impacted by minor but emotionally compelling challenges, such as a change of membership.

Growing Your Leadership Resilience

Leadership Resilience: Momentous Active

If your score in this part of the questionnaire is lower than zero, take some time to think about how you respond to the hurdles your organization encounters when pursuing major projects. Your responses suggest that you may perceive such hurdles as intense blows to your confidence as a leader. This may mean that you refuse to acknowledge their severity, that you assign blame too easily, or that you leap to solutions before fully understanding the problems. It's natural to want to shut out momentous challenges. Perhaps most of us do this to an extent. To develop your leadership resilience, however, explore the following:

- Open up to the people you lead. Share your vision with them, not only in words but also by acknowledging and sharing their emotional and cognitive burdens. Make it clear to the people you lead that their contributions matter.

- Share power and authority with people you trust. Delegate more. One caveat, however: resist the urge to delegate as a way to avoid difficult and time-consuming tasks. Use delegation as a way to improve the functioning of your organization and stay committed to supporting the people who take on the tasks, both emotionally and cognitively. Be more inclusive. When you invite those whom you lead to take ownership and show agency, you may be surprised by the qualities they demonstrate.

If your score in this section is positive, you probably have a solid foundation for managing active momentous challenges. Every momentous challenge is unique, so:

- Continue to develop your leadership approach. Resist the urge to ignore signals that make you uncomfortable. Share your leadership resources, recognize the value of your colleagues' contributions, and avoid elitism.

Leadership Resilience: Momentous Reactive

If your score in this area dipped below zero, it appears that sudden shocks to your projects tend to affect your leadership equilibrium. Perhaps you struggle to acknowledge the scale of any challenges you encounter, attempting to delay your response or even avoid dealing with them altogether. In practice, it's likely that these tactics will only delay the inevitable day of reckoning, while damaging your ability to provide emotional and cognitive resources to those whom you lead.

What should you do instead? Consider these options:

- Accept momentous challenges head-on. They are integral to success, and you cannot avoid them. If you try to protect yourself by ignoring the risks, this is a sign that you are depleted emotionally and cognitively. Note your response. If you start blaming others, this represents a retreat from your role as leader and suggests that your reserves of leadership resilience are very low.

- Again, engaging a coach can be helpful in these circumstances. As a leader, it's essential that you cultivate accountability. With no one above you in your organization, you may need to create this for yourself.

If your score in this section is positive, it's likely that your leadership resilience is reasonably strong. Nonetheless, you may consider this:

- Follow the advice described in previous sections to maintain and further develop your leadership resilience.

Leadership Resilience: Trivial Active

If your score in this section of the questionnaire needs improvement, reflect on how you as a leader respond to the trivial challenges that arise when you strive to create change. These challenges may nag at you and distract you from your objectives, draining your emotional energy as a leader.

To address these challenges, try the following:

- Recognize that they are trivial. Understand that in the context of your larger goals, they are relatively minor.

- Therefore, help your organization see them in the proper perspective. Engage with them at your own convenience instead of allowing them to dictate to you.

- If necessary, hire a trusted coach to provide you with feedback and guidance. Leadership can be a lonely mantle to bear, so give yourself the support you need to remain focused.

If your score in this section of the questionnaire is positive, it's likely that you have some reserves of resilience you can draw on to meet the trivial challenges that come your way. If this is the case, your task is to maintain and build on those reserves. Consider the following:

- Imagine your organization as a car driving down a road with numerous potholes. Your leadership resilience equates to your capacity to help your organization navigate those potholes. The more resilience you have, the more emotional and cognitive resources you can provide your organization with along the bumpy road ahead.

- Maintaining and growing your resilience will allow you to sustain the levels of emotional and cognitive resources you'll need to lead others. Stay alert and look out for surprises that could drain your organization's resilience. The more quickly you see the signs, the more likely it is that you can avoid getting stuck and spinning your emotional and cognitive wheels.

Leadership Resilience: Trivial Reactive

If your score in this section of the questionnaire is lower than zero, it indicates that you may be easily influenced by the small challenges you face as a leader. Although these challenges may not be particularly relevant to your objectives, they may occupy a disproportionate amount of your attention. Perhaps you even question your ability to lead effectively. To address this issue, consider the following:

- Trivial challenges may *seem* important, but objectively they make a minor contribution to your organization's overall success. Find ways of putting them into perspective, for example by seeking feedback from trusted friends or a coach.

- Think of overinvolvement in trivial challenges as a slippery slope. The more quickly you can identify the signs and take action, the more likely it is that you'll be able to address the decline before it has a significant impact on your business.

If your score in this section of the questionnaire is positive, you probably have some level of resilience to draw on in the face of reactive trivial challenges. Nonetheless, bear the following in mind:

- Resilience can easily deteriorate when it is not actively cultivated. What are you doing to deliberately develop your resilience? This may include practices that you find valuable and talking to people you trust, for example a coach.

Revisiting This Questionnaire

As we hope we've demonstrated throughout this book, resilience is a flexible quality. Your answers today represent a snapshot of your resilience. They can and will change over time.

The best way to use this questionnaire is as a tool to regularly assess your resilience. Revisit it in a couple of months, and you may find that the results are completely different. Do this repeatedly and you will build up a picture of the way your resilience fluctuates, including the types of influence that drain it and those that support you in becoming more resilient.

You can use these results to inform your decision-making. Choose to participate in activities that build your resilience, and engage with people who support the development of your resilience. As you grow in self-understanding, you will have the knowledge to make better choices. This doesn't mean that your life will be free of challenge, of course, only that you will be in a position to meet your challenges more effectively.

With the insights you have gleaned from learning about your own resilience, you may wish to reread some of the stories from earlier chapters. What do you see now that you didn't see before? How has your perception of resilience shifted as you have read this book?

Whatever form of resilience you wish to grow—individual, team, or leadership—remember that it starts with you. Only when you know yourself can you be of service to others. Make a commitment to practices that support your resilience, and then use the firm foundations of those practices to develop your stability and compassion.

Key Takeaways from This Chapter

- If you read this book without doing the exercises, you will only gain half the benefits. It's great to understand resilience in general, but it's even better to know your *own* resilience.

- Resilience is not fixed. By understanding your existing resilience levels, you can pinpoint the areas in which you most need to grow.

- You may be highly resilient in some areas of your life, while lacking resilience in other areas. That's okay. Now that you know this, you can make informed decisions about what to prioritize.

- Continually revisit this questionnaire to chart changes in your resilience. When you understand the circumstances that influence your resilience, both positively and negatively, you can nurture it more effectively.

CONCLUSION

AS WE DRAW THIS BOOK TO A CLOSE, WE'D LIKE TO THANK YOU FOR joining us on the journey.

Perhaps there have been moments along the road when you have wondered why "resilience," a word that has been part of the English language for a long time, has recently attracted so much research and discussion.

If you stop and consider how our lives today compare with those of our ancestors, you will surely conclude that they required far more resilience than we do. History, both ancient and modern, relates plenty of disasters, privation, and challenges that have tested human resilience to its very limits, sometimes beyond.

Compared to the hardships previous generations have endured, we are relatively fortunate. You may or may not agree with Professor Steven Pinker's contention that life is getting better for most people,[38] but it's undeniable that the present day compares favorably with previous ages in which life was "nasty, brutish, and short."[39] If this is the case, why has interest in resilience undergone such a surge?

One response to this question is that as our understanding of how we handle challenges improves, we have more to say about the subject. Ours is a proactive age, in which we aspire constantly to do better. This ambition stretches our emotional and cognitive resources to their limits. Understanding resilience provides us with valuable insights, which

---

38 Steven Pinker, *Enlightenment Now: The Case for Reason, Science, Humanism, and Progress* (New York: Penguin, 2018).

39 Glen Newey, *The Routledge Guidebook to Hobbes' Leviathan* (Oxford: Routledge, 2014).

can help us make good decisions and avoid bad decisions as we work to achieve our objectives.

Ours is also an age of unprecedented mobility. We move from one job to another, and one place to another, far more often than did previous generations. This tendency means that we experience far more change than previous generations. Change is stressful and challenging, even when the intended outcome is positive. Therefore, the number of changes we willingly make to our lives greatly increases the probability that we will have to cope with both momentous and trivial challenges, both those of our own making and those that we encounter unexpectedly. If we wish to live successfully in a dynamic, rapidly changing environment, it is essential that we know and grow our resilience.

There's another very important reason why change invites us all to focus on our resilience. We live in an age in which our conception of the future is more advanced than ever before. Whatever we are doing in our day-to-day lives, we all understand that change, both in our individual lives and in the wider world, is a constant possibility.

We are future-oriented creatures who wish to predict and respond to change as quickly as it arrives—perhaps even more quickly. In previous generations, news was slow to arrive and usually came from one of a few trusted sources. As long as we kept ourselves informed, we felt able to make contingency plans and take precautions.

Life may have been tough at times, but we lived with less daily uncertainty. We expended fewer emotional and cognitive resources in contemplating the broad range of possible scenarios that might come to pass. Today, we can turn on the television, visit a favorite website, log on to Facebook, or read the latest retweet from a friend, and we will quickly be inundated with news of change that is happening right now or may happen soon.

When we contemplate such a broad range of possible futures, and when we find ourselves so frequently needing to make decisions about which ones to pursue and which to discard, our anxieties about whether we are choosing the right options naturally intensify. In this environment, we need resilience both to meet our immediate challenges and to decide whether we should prepare to meet potential challenges, which may or may not ever happen.

To do this effectively calls for another dimension of resilience: resilience that can most accurately be described as *predictive*. We must make decisions about where to focus our attention and continually adapt that focus in light of new information. This form of resilience requires us to bounce back emotionally and cognitively from threats that may appear deceptively real, even when they don't actually materialize.

In writing this book, we have primarily discussed the resilience that has the greatest impact in this moment. As we draw it to a close, however, we hope that you will apply the lessons contained within these pages in a broader context whenever you find yourself struggling to deal with the avalanche of information that rushes unbidden into your life on a daily basis.

We sometimes hear people talk about resilience as though it's a binary concept, a quality we either have or lack. We firmly disagree with this perspective. It's certainly possible to develop resilience. Indeed, history tells us that entire populations can discover hitherto undreamed-of reserves of resilience in the face of economic depressions or the privations of war.

The good news is that, with practice, we can all develop our reserves of resilience, no matter our external circumstances. This is not always an easy or comfortable process. It is similar to taking up or returning to exercise. If you were never much of an athlete, or if you haven't trained for many years, your first visit to the gym won't work miracles. Quite the reverse, in fact: you will probably wake up the next day in a great deal of pain. If you train regularly for six months, however, you will begin to see an appreciable difference in your strength and fitness. Resilience is much the same. Only by regularly engaging our resilience can we see what a difference it makes to our daily lives.

Our aim in these pages has been to deliver both a conceptual understanding of resilience and to give you a practical way to address your own resilience. We want you to close this book thinking of resilience as far more than an increasingly popular buzzword, frequently used but not always clearly defined.

We hope that the stories we've told you have engaged your imagination and given you a conceptual framework you can use to recognize the key qualities of a resilient decision-maker. As a result, we trust that you have a greater understanding of how different types of challenges require different types of resilience. In tandem with those stories, we'd like to think that the exercises we've designed have enabled you to see your own resilience, and your own potential for improvement, more clearly.

It's important to remember that resilience doesn't always grow of its own accord. It often requires a conscious effort. To make the best possible use of the information you've gleaned from taking the questionnaire in chapter 7, we suggest that you set yourself resilience targets. What active challenges do you foresee in the next few months? What can you do to boost your resilience so that, a year from now, you will be stronger and more capable of meeting challenges? Are there specific *types* of challenges you need to address more competently? We encourage you to reread this book in six months or a year and to reflect on resilience from your new vantage point.

Growing resilience can sometimes be a lonely road. If you find your motivation depleting, it's often valuable to discuss your experiences with people you trust. Perhaps you have friends or colleagues with whom you can do this, or perhaps you will wish to hire a coach or adviser. Whomever you choose to speak to, it's important that they know you well and that they are both willing and able to support the development of your resilience.

As you walk this path, it's vitally important that you remain honest with yourself. When dealing with challenges, we all experience the urge to avoid unpleasant truths about ourselves. The only time we truly grow, however, is when we find the courage to admit to our strengths and weaknesses. When we can acknowledge our overreactions and anxieties, when we can hold our hands up and say, "I could have handled that better," we are truly growing resilience.

A final note: resilience is an evolving field. If you'd like to stay up-to-date with the latest insights, visit our website: *www.theresilientdecisionmaker.com*. We'll be happy to share quality research with you as it emerges and support you as you walk the path of knowing and growing your resilience.

ACKNOWLEDGMENTS

Joseph Lampel

While writing about resilience, I have inevitably noticed the people in my life who have made it possible for me to hang on and to go further than I imagined possible. My first lessons in resilience came from my parents, although I did not know it at the time because they spoke so rarely about what they had endured. Anne-Marie has lent me her support when it has mattered most, with considerable forbearance and good humor. I have needed to be resilient for my daughter, Estelle, as she has gone through the ups and downs of growing up. She, in turn, has been resilient for me, often reassuring me by saying, "Don't worry, Dad, everything is going to be all right!"

I owe a great deal to my friends and co-authors, Ajay and Aneesh. This book was their idea. Looking back, I am amazed at how calm and collected they have remained throughout the journey, keeping me on track while I have seesawed between optimism and pessimism. My brother, Michael, who never gives up, has served as a splendid model of resilience. Whether they know it or not, my friends Robert, Amalya, Benson, and Caroline have given me courage, and Daniel, my staunch ally and friend, has always been there, willing to listen and help.

Aneesh Banerjee

A number of people have been instrumental in this journey, notably my co-authors, colleagues, and friends. Joseph and Ajay have been my intellectual partners in this project. Divya, as always, has been the steady voice of reason, while Aunoy has been an advocate for the reader. My wonderful parents have provided unconditional support and the several students, friends, and family who have been my sounding board for some of the ideas in this book have been most helpful and incredibly patient. Thank you!

Ajay Bhalla

It's nothing profound to note that the great things in life tend to show up unanticipated. Certainly, this is the case with my deep friendship with Joseph Lampel and Aneesh Banerjee. Without Joseph and Aneesh, this book would have not come to life.

Twenty-one years ago, I read Joseph's first book, *Strategy Safari*, while pursuing my doctoral studies. At the time, I didn't have the faintest idea that I would one day have the good fortune of working with him. Joseph and I joined Cass Business School one year apart, but it would be another two years before we met by chance while walking one evening to an Underground station in London. That ten-minute interaction has led to a deeply meaningful lifelong relationship spanning multiple projects. Joseph is a fountain of knowledge with an exceptional capacity to see problems through a range of different lenses and weave those varying perspectives together coherently. I have relied on his wise counsel to see through the forest on countless occasions. Joseph, you have been a wonderful guide and colleague. Thank you.

Likewise, my first meeting with Aneesh, eleven years ago, was pure serendipity. We met while interviewing a board member of SAP AG in Walldorf, Germany. Little did I know then that he would become such a close colleague. Over the years, and especially while working on this book, I have been truly impressed with Aneesh's laser-sharp ability to see through massive amounts of information and give seemingly disparate ideas a logical order. A man wise beyond his years, his friendship has been a gift I dearly cherish.

My contributions in this book would not have been possible without the insights of my students and executives, who seek my advice in both business and personal matters and place enormous trust in me.

I am very grateful to have had three amazing people in my life, all of whom were living embodiments of resilience in their personal and professional lives. The first was my uncle, Ram Murti Chopra, who was my guru and lived his life as a saint. He taught me the power of karma and loving kindness.

The other two sadly passed away during the writing of this book, testing my personal resilience to its limits. The first was my loving brother-in-law, Sukhdev Maini, a man who deployed his business as a tool to serve humanity and who taught me the power of humility and righteousness. The second was my nephew, Anuj Chopra, who passed away unexpectedly at the age of thirty. Anuj introduced me to the power of perseverance, reminding me constantly not to be swept away by hurdles but instead to focus on what we can build in this precious lifetime. A living symbol of positive self-belief, Anuj was blessed with a brilliant mind. While pursuing his doctoral studies at Imperial College, he focused on developing an AI-powered traffic management system for flying vehicles. Following a decision not to join the British intelligence services, he built a multimillion-dollar global business in less than five years. His genius and insight into life left a deep imprint on me.

A great debt of gratitude is reserved for my wonderful family. My parents, Kuldip and Raj, have supported me unfailingly with the gift of their love. They have been twin pillars of strength in my life. They taught me the art of resilience by example through displaying so much resilience when life threw all the challenges it possibly could at them. I'd also like to thank my sister, Anju, brother-in-law, Dinesh, and niece, Pallavi, for their unconditional love and support.

Above all, I'm deeply grateful to my wife, Bhavna, for being a force of selflessness and humbleness; and my daughters, Khushi and Arya, and my son, Raghuvir, who never fail to make me smile, give me purpose, and remind me of what matters most. The abundant love and belief with which they provide me fills every day of my life with sunshine and the desire to make a positive difference in this world.

ABOUT THE AUTHORS

Joseph Lampel obtained his doctorate from McGill University in Montreal, Canada, before taking up his first academic position at the Stern School of Business, New York University. Today, Joseph holds the Eddie Davies Professorship in Enterprise and Innovation Management at the Alliance Manchester Business School, part of the University of Manchester.

Joseph has published more than fifty articles in a wide range of academic and practitioner journals, from the *Academy of Management Journal* to the *MIT Sloan Management Review*. He has also written for the mainstream business press, notably *Fortune* and the *Financial Times*. He has published six books, of which the best known is *Strategy Safari: A Guided Tour Through the Wilds of Strategic Management*, co-authored with Henry Mintzberg and Bruce Ahlstrand.

Over the years, Joseph has consulted and worked with a broad range of organizations, most prominently John Lewis Partnership, EMI Music Group, GlaxoSmithKline, the International Chamber of Commerce, and the Employee Ownership Association.

Aneesh Banerjee researches, consults, and lectures on business strategy, technology, and innovation management. He's currently an assistant professor at Cass Business School, City, University of London.

His research has been recognized by the Academy of Management and the International Society for Professional Innovation Management (ISPIM). One of Aneesh's keenest interests is employee-owned businesses, firms in which employees own a significant and meaningful stake in the business. Passionate about cultural and creative industries, Aneesh is currently chair of the British Academy of Management (BAM) conference's Cultural and Creative Industries (CCI) track.

Aneesh's teaching has been recognized through a number of awards, including the Chancellor's Award—City, University of London's highest award in recognition of excellence in learning and teaching.

He gained his undergraduate degree in physics at St. Stephen's College in Delhi, his MBA from the Xavier School of Management (XLRI) in Jamshedpur, Jharkhand, and his master's in research and PhD from Cass Business School at City, University of London.

Born into a third-generation family business in India, **Ajay Bhalla** grew up listening to stories of his grandfather first being ejected from a business he co-founded, then responding by building a second, successful family business.

This naturally led Ajay to a fascination with the topic of entrepreneurial family businesses—an area in which he pursued his doctoral studies. Since 2001, Ajay has worked at Cass Business School, part of City, University of London, where he currently holds the Professorship in Family Business and Innovation.

Over the years, Ajay has published several top academic articles and won multiple awards for his executive teaching and research. He has also worked with his co-authors on developing an understanding of links between ownership and resilience.

Today, Ajay is deeply passionate about helping senior executives and organizations recognize how they can become more resilient. He sits on the board of the Institute for Family Business Research Foundation, which represents some of the largest multigenerational family businesses in the United Kingdom.

Printed in Great
Britain
by Amazon